No More Invisible Man

- Hegmonic - ideal
- Complicit - monitor mea
- Sub - gay
  - marg - disadvant
      min

Assertive

No More Invisible Man

Race and Gender in Men's Work

Adia Harvey Wingfield

TEMPLE UNIVERSITY PRESS
Philadelphia

TEMPLE UNIVERSITY PRESS
Philadelphia, Pennsylvania 19122
www.temple.edu/tempress

Copyright © 2013 by Temple University
All rights reserved
Published 2013

Library of Congress Cataloging-in-Publication Data

Wingfield, Adia Harvey, 1977–
    No more invisible man : race and gender in men's work / Adia
Harvey Wingfield.
        p. cm.
    Includes bibliographical references and index.
    ISBN 978-1-4399-0972-0 (cloth : alk. paper) —
ISBN 978-1-4399-0973-7 (pbk. : alk. paper) —
ISBN 978-1-4399-0974-4 (e-book)   1. African Americans in the
professions.   2. African American professional employees.
3. African American men—Employment.   4. Discrimination in
employment—United States.   5. Glass ceiling (Employment
discrimination)—United States.   I. Title.
    HD8038.U5W564 2013
    331.6'396073—dc23
                                                    2012014650

Printed in the United States of America

121313P

Contents

Acknowledgments

I owe a debt of gratitude to many people who helped me at various stages of this project.

I dedicate this book to the two most important and influential men in my life: my father, William Harvey, who was my first model for what a great man should be, and my husband, John Harvey Wingfield, who every day meets the high standards that were set in my formative years. I am so fortunate to have a father who is and has always been an exemplary role model and to have an incredible husband who makes every day a great day. I also thank the following people in my network for providing critical emotional and social support: my mother, Brenda Harvey, who is always my biggest cheerleader, and my sister, Amina Harvey, who inspires me to strive to do and to be better. Thanks go to Brandon Wingfield for being a good kid with a positive attitude about life. And thanks go to my baby girl, Johari Wingfield, for coming into and enriching our lives immeasurably. I am also grateful for the unbreakable bonds I share with Ashley Brown, Karmen Davis, Kamola Gray, Felicia Jackson, and Dee Stiff-Roberts, and I thank them for being my BFFs.

In my professional life, I have had the fortune to receive feedback from several colleagues who kindly and generously helped me improve the manuscript. I thank Jennifer Pierce, Christine Williams, Joya Misra, and Joe Feagin, who reviewed several versions of this work. I am also grateful to Kevin Williams, Roger Kamau, Raheem Beyah, and Rebecca Romo Weir, who offered key assistance in the development of this project, and Kelsey Schwarz, who provided invaluable help when it came time to put the finishing touches on the manuscript. I also thank Mick Gusinde-Duffy for his enthusiastic support of this project.

Finally, I thank all the men who generously gave their time and energy to help me complete this book. I hope that I have succeeded in telling their stories honestly and accurately.

No More Invisible Man

Introduction

R alph Ellison's classic novel *Invisible Man* examines the life of an unnamed black male protagonist to provide social commentary about the impact of racism in U.S. society. By depicting the title character as socially rather than physically invisible, Ellison pointedly critiques not only the mechanisms of racism that cast black Americans as stereotyped representations rather than fully developed, complex human beings but also the ways that blacks can become marginalized if they fail to fit the stereotyped depictions. Yet simultaneously, Ellison's narrator comes to observe and appreciate some of the benefits of invisibility. Thus, by using this metaphor, Ellison skillfully explores the multidimensional dynamics racial inequality creates for black men.

Ellison's novel is critically acclaimed largely because it accurately conveys the emotions and frustrations that many black Americans experience, particularly when they do not conform to broader stereotypes of race. Indeed, blacks who do not fit cultural representations of "blackness" are overlooked, dismissed, or otherwise rendered invisible in ways that reflect the processes Ellison describes. This is particularly true when it comes to black men, especially those whose images conflict with the two most common current cultural depictions of black masculinity.

On one hand, many media outlets, news reports, and other sources document the challenges and obstacles facing black men who are part of the "urban underclass." The *Washington Post*'s 2006 series *Being a Black Man* offers multiple narratives of black men trapped in the criminal justice system (at least one case a result of mistaken identity) or facing poverty, illness, and overall despair.[1] Sociological research tends to fall into this camp, with numerous studies having done their part to keep attention focused on these issues. Studies of black men typically examine their challenging experiences in the urban underclass, their low performance in the educational system, their overrepresentation in the criminal justice system, or their general feelings of malaise and detachment from the broader society.[2] Often, these studies offer empirical validation of the stories that appear in the news media. Documenting the very real challenges and obstacles facing many black men in contemporary American society, they represent these men as marginalized, dispossessed, alienated from mainstream society, and underserved by most major social institutions.

On the other hand, contrasting representations of black men generally reflect the realities of those who are part of an elite group. These black men are highly educated and often extremely wealthy, and their success reveals, directly or indirectly, a path to upward mobility. President Barack Obama and Bill Cosby, for example, are emblematic of this alternative representation of black men in contemporary America. As a multimillionaire entertainer and philanthropist, Cosby represents an image that is diametrically opposed to the depictions of poverty, illness, joblessness, and crime. In contrast, Cosby embodies success, wealth, and power that seems to negate the existence of racial issues for black men and seems to suggest that those who work hard and adopt culturally appropriate values can achieve success. Indeed, in a 2004 speech at Howard University, at several subsequent speaking engagements, and in a 2007 book decrying black victimization, Cosby delivered this very message.[3]

Ultimately, these accounts suggest a very two-dimensional picture of black men's lives in the United States today. The casual observer may assume that nearly *all* black men are facing the dire threats of un- or underemployment, failing schools, and jail time. At the other end of the continuum, the high visibility of the extremely well-off minority serves to downplay the suggestion that structural issues persist in significantly shaping life chances and social outcomes. To date, little media attention, research, or analysis has been focused on other aspects of black men's experiences.

The men who fall between these two poles are the "invisible men" examined in this book. According to the Bureau of Labor Statistics, 25 percent of black men are employed in professional/managerial jobs.[4] However, black professional men's occupational experiences are very rarely the subject of sociological research and analysis. For these men, in contrast to their working-class or working-poor counterparts, issues of unemployment, marginalization from mainstream society, and an over-zealous criminal justice system may not be their most pressing social problems. When it comes to employment and labor market opportunities, black professional men may assign more urgency to issues related to promotion, mobility, and the development of occupational networks. Additionally, these issues may be compounded—or at the very least affected—by the occupational composition of the jobs in which these men are most likely to be concentrated. Because jobs remain mostly sex segregated, men and women are concentrated in different occupations, with men in the majority as construction workers, architects, and correctional officers and women in the majority as nurses, teachers, and library staff.[5] The gendered composition of jobs may affect the types of issues that black professional men encounter at work.

The work experiences of black professional men are of sociological importance because they can help us gain insight into issues of power and inequality in the workplace. Black professional men inhabit an interesting location wherein they receive social and economic advantages by virtue of their gender and class but suffer disadvantages that result from racial inequality. As such, their experiences are qualitatively different from those of their black female counterparts, from those of white women, and from those of men of other racial groups. Sociologist Patricia Hill Collins notes that studying how these categories intersect is more than an intellectual exercise; considering the intersections of race, gender, and class contributes to our understanding that the subtle machinations of power, domination, and subordination work in complex ways for various groups.[6] A focus on black professional men, then, helps to elucidate the particulars of how inequality affects men when they experience simultaneous privilege and disadvantage.

Black men who work in predominantly white male professional environments are likely to encounter specific challenges and opportunities that differ from not only those facing black men who are members of the underclass but also those facing black women who are in professional jobs. But little research has examined what these issues may be or how they are manifested. Research on black professionals suggests that they can encounter difficulties developing the necessary social ties that facilitate advancement, but are these obstacles exacerbated or minimized for black men who work primarily with other men? Studies of black women professionals indicate that intersections of race and gender subject them to specific stereotypes that hinder their occupational success, but what images and representations impact black men in the professional workplace? To what extent do they feel hindered or constrained by these depictions? What general challenges do black men encounter in these work environments, and how are these issues shaped by the status of being black men working in a white male–dominated, professional setting?

No More Invisible Man attempts to address these and other questions. Drawing from several sociological theories, I assess how black professional men describe the challenges, opportunities, interactions, and other issues that characterize their work in white male–dominated jobs. I consider how intersections of race and gender affect black men's lives in the occupational arena and highlight the ways these overlapping factors shape their experiences with tokenization. Thus, this book provides a sociological view of how tokenism varies depending on the ways that race and gender intersect for social actors, the occupational challenges that persist in the workplace, and, more broadly, the frequently overlooked issues that affect black men.

In Chapter 1, I discuss and review the theoretical arguments that guide this study. The chapter details the theory of tokenism, how it has developed over the years, and the areas where additional research is still needed.[7] In Chapter 1, I also review the concept of gendered organizations and its theoretical contributions to this book.[8] Finally, I highlight the literature on black professionals that reveals some of the issues black men face and the failure of this literature to contextualize the issues in terms of the concept of gendered occupations or intersections of race and gender. I draw from the literature to introduce the concept of partial tokenization—the theoretical paradigm guiding this book—arguing that intersections of race, class, and gender, coupled with work in a gendered occupation, put black professional men in a position of partial tokenization.

In subsequent chapters, I flesh out the concept of partial tokenization. Chapter 2 outlines the broad challenges facing these men and the challenges that are reflective of being black in predominantly white occupations. I discuss the men's descriptions of the general obstacles, issues, and problems they encounter in their jobs, and I examine the ways in which these challenges reflect the concept of partial tokenization.[9]

Chapter 3 focuses on black men's descriptions of their interactions with women in the workplace. Black men in white male–dominated jobs hold an interesting position relative to their female coworkers. Black men are in the racial minority in these occupations, but white women are in the gender minority. Black women and other women of color, in contrast, face challenges that accrue from disadvantages related to both race and gender. Thus, in Chapter 3, I consider black men's descriptions of their interactions and relationships with both groups of women. I examine how black men engage with other numerical minorities and explore the ways these interactions are shaped by the process of partial tokenism.

Chapter 4 assesses how black men interact with other men in their jobs. The theory of tokenization I discuss analyzes how those in the minority interact with one another as a result of the behaviors enacted by the dominant group. I use partial tokenization to offer a more precise interpretation of black men's interactions with other men. This theoretical development helps to explain not only the relationships of these men with other black men but also the nuanced interactions that they forge and maintain with white male colleagues and supervisors. I find that, as with women, black men's interactions with other men are more complex than the theory of tokenism allows.

In Chapter 5, I build on some of the ideas advanced in the preceding two chapters to examine how the men in this study construct performances of masculinity. Here, I review the literature on masculinity, how masculinity is performed in occupational contexts, and how it reflects the concept of gendered occupations. I argue that partial tokenization informs the stereotyped informal roles to which these men are subjected and that intersections of race and gender inform the types of marginalized masculinities they construct as a result.

Chapter 6 tackles the question of emotional labor within gendered occupations and how it is performed when a worker experiences racial tokenization. This chapter draws on both the concept of emotional labor and resulting studies that consider the performance of emotion work in gendered occupations, such as litigation, police work, and sales.[10] I build on these studies to examine how partial tokenization complicates the performance of the emotion work black professional men do to navigate the largely white male–dominated work worlds they inhabit.

Finally, the Conclusion reviews the key arguments and central points offered, shows how the arguments presented contribute to and further develop the existing research, and proposes future research and policy implications.

1 | Tokenism Reassessed

Today, the image of black professional men is one that rarely sparks surprise or shock. On television, black men have been depicted in professional occupations ranging from judges (*Law and Order*) to national security agents (*24*) to presidents (*The Event*). In real life, black men are indeed judges, security agents, and presidents—they also work as accountants, consultants, news analysts, and college professors, among many other occupations. Yet despite their increasing presence, they are often in the numerical minority in their work environments. They also face invisibility, with many people assuming that, despite positive fictional representations on television, most black men are part of a criminal underclass. In this book, I highlight the experiences of black male professionals to illustrate the challenges, obstacles, and opportunities they encounter in their jobs.

I draw from several sociological theories that help give shape to black men's experiences. I rely on Rosabeth Moss Kanter's theory of tokenism to assess the ways workers face particular challenges when they are members of a numerical minority. Also, I use Joan Acker's theory of gendered organizations and occupations to highlight how tokenization varies depending on the gender of both the worker and the occupation.[1] Further, I review the literature on black professionals to show how it not only reflects some of Kanter's arguments but also reveals some limitations to her theoretical analysis. Finally, I use intersectional theory to show why it is important to assess the interactions of race, class, and gender in analyzing black professional men's occupational lives. These theoretical paradigms offer a solid foundation for assessing black men's social interactions, performances, and opportunities in certain professions.

Tokenism

In her classic work *Men and Women of the Corporation*, Kanter develops the theory of tokenism to explain the occupational dynamics she observes among executives in a major company.[2] Studying the differences between high-ranking male and female employees, Kanter observes that women's experiences often diverge sharply from those of their male counterparts. In general, she contends that "the proportional rarity of tokens is associated with three perceptual tendencies: visibility, contrast, and assimilation."[3] *Visibility* refers to the ways in which women stand out in the workplace by virtue of their low numbers, leading to *performance pressures* that create an odd sense of both conspicuousness and invisibility. *Contrast* describes the processes by which members of the majority attempt to highlight the differences between themselves and those in the minority; it can be observed when dominant groups exaggerate *dominant culture boundaries*, leaving those in the minority isolated. Ultimately, this leads them to turn against one another and demonstrate loyalty to the dominant group. Finally, *assimilation* involves how the majority uses stereotypes to evaluate the minority, giving rise to *role encapsulation*, wherein individuals are seen first and foremost as representatives of their group rather than as discrete human beings who maintain a certain status. Kanter argues that these factors create standards, occupational experiences, and social interactions for women in the corporation that are different from those of their male counterparts. Ultimately, as a result of these perceptual tendencies, tokens are more likely to be stereotyped, isolated, and generally regarded as incompetent.

Based on these observations, Kanter concludes that those in the numerical minority experience "tokenization."[4] The token experience causes these women to experience the professional workplace differently from their male counterparts. Tokenization creates additional work, barriers, and challenges for women of the corporation, as they are forced to prove themselves to their male colleagues, act to offset stereotypes, and generally struggle to be viewed and treated as competent, capable professionals. It establishes a work environment that is unequally skewed in favor of the male workers, whose numerical advantage allows them to enjoy opportunities for social networking and mentoring, and even latitude for error, that are not available to the female professionals.

Ultimately, Kanter concludes that the token experience stems from numerical representation. She contends that women's low numbers at the upper levels of the organization facilitate the perceptual tendencies she identifies. However, while Kanter identifies this process as occurring mostly among women, she argues that tokenization is not necessarily gender driven. In fact, Kanter theorizes that *anyone* in the numerical minority of a group experiences similar social processes. As such, she presents a broad, general theory of tokenization that purports to identify and explain the mechanisms that maintain inequality whenever there are unequal representations among different groups.

This aspect of Kanter's argument is important because it downplays questions of power and hegemony that members of various groups may carry into their token experiences. In other words, Kanter's theory suggests that the process of tokenism will have the same impact regardless of whether the group dynamics involve a white male in the numerical minority relative to black women, a Latina in the numerical minority relative to white men, or an Asian American woman relative to Asian American men. Kanter contends that, in a given setting, being in the minority leads to a rather common, generalized experience that includes marginalization, hypervisibility and invisibility, stereotyping, and isolation. According to her framework, those in the majority have the power to impart these processes onto those in the minority.

Since the publication of Kanter's work, researchers have examined more closely this question of whether the token experience is generalizable across the board regardless of the background of the token. To this day, studies still build on Kanter's framework to assess the particularities of tokenism. Most research has suggested that Kanter overstates the extent to which tokenization occurs in a parallel fashion for all tokens.[5] In contrast, these studies indicate that the social groups to which tokens belong can have a marked impact on shaping the token experience.

Depending on the characteristics of the tokenized group, the experience of tokenization can lead to the reproduction of larger social patterns of stratification, inequality, and disparities that actually work in the group's favor. Or the process of tokenization can inhibit numerical minorities' opportunities for upward mobility and occupational ascension.

Research on gender in the workplace offers some of the most important studies that further develop and highlight the complexities of the token experience. These studies offer empirical evidence that runs counter to Kanter's assertion about the uniformity of the token experience. In particular, these studies draw differences between the experiences of male and female tokens in various work environments. By virtue of their maleness, men are members of a privileged social group (though the advantages this bestows are not shared equally among all men). Therefore, men's experiences with tokenization when they are in the minority among women do not necessarily mirror what women encounter in the same position. Men's higher status, prestige, and social standing accompany them into the token position, providing them with a very different minority experience than that of women.

Token Women in "Male" Jobs

Many of the studies about token women that follow Kanter's research draw conclusions that are consistent with her original theorizations. For example, Lilian Floge and Deborah Merrill's study of the medical profession finds that women physicians face many of the same problems Kanter identifies.[6] Women doctors encounter the perception that they lack the qualifications, skills, and talents to perform their duties effectively. Conversely, their male counterparts rarely describe facing this kind of prejudice from colleagues, patients, or supervisors. This finding is consistent with the numerical breakdown of women employed as doctors at the time, which was during the mid-1980s. Floge and Merrill contend that women were a small percentage of the doctors in the hospital, thus rendering them a visible numerical minority that experienced tokenized treatment.[7]

Louise Roth's more recent book, *Selling Women Short*, yields similar conclusions.[8] Roth's work is an analysis of women workers on Wall Street. Though she does not explicitly use Kanter's token analysis, Roth shows that women employed on Wall Street are subjected to some of the same perceptual tendencies (heightened visibility, struggles to assimilate) that Kanter argues are endemic to the token experience.[9] As with the women respondents in Floge and Merrill's study, women on Wall Street work in a highly masculinized environment.[10] Most of their colleagues are men, and Wall Street culture has been widely identified as a hypermasculine environment where women may be described and treated as sexual objects. Furthermore, office policies may be unfriendly to women (particularly mothers), and behaviors and attitudes associated with femininity may be derided.[11] Thus, Roth's findings that women on Wall Street can feel highly visible, experience ostracism and difficulty finding mentors, and face negative stereotypes further support Kanter's token theory.[12]

Kris Paap's ethnographic analysis of women in the construction industry offers another perspective to confirm Kanter's claims.[13] In working construction, Paap finds further evidence of women being marginalized, denied opportunities, and isolated from male peers and colleagues.[14] In working as an apprentice on a construction site, Paap cites specific cases of fellow workers who sexualize her through references to her breasts, thus highlighting the contrast between the men and herself. She also describes greater difficulty getting work projects that lead to advancement compared with her male colleagues, showing how women in this field are isolated from the majority and reinforcing the idea that women are not truly capable of doing construction work. Overall, Paap describes an occupational environment that erects added obstacles for women.

Paap's work is similar to that of Floge and Merrill as well as that of Roth in the sense that she corroborates Kanter's conclusions about the effects of being in the numerical minority.[15] However, her work diverges from these earlier studies because it centers on a different occupational population. While Floge and Merrill, along with Roth, assess the token experience among workers in white-collar jobs, Paap's attention is on the ways that these processes actually help working-class white men maintain a sense of security in an industry that is rapidly changing and becoming less solid as an option for skilled workers.[16] The significance of this is that Paap's study shows how the process of tokenization—specifically, working to tokenize minorities—may help members of the majority feel better about any loss of status or prestige they might experience.[17] Taken together, these three studies paint a vivid picture of the myriad challenges and obstacles some women face when they experience tokenization from the male majority.

Token Men in "Women's" Professions

While the research on women's experiences in male-dominated fields is consistent with Kanter's arguments, other studies offer different conclusions.[18] In particular, the research on men who do "women's work" offers a pointed critique of Kanter's claim that the token experience is universal and broadly shared by the numerical minority. These studies consider Kanter's basic premise of tokenism but examine situations that reverse her original observations, which are based on a study of women who were in the numerical minority at a major corporation. Later research considers the experiences men have when they are in the numerical minority in various occupations but finds very different results.

Studies in this vein highlight Joan Acker's theory of gendered organizations and occupations as a critical aspect of understanding how the token experience can work differently for various groups.[19] In her influential article "Hierarchies, Jobs, Bodies," Acker argues that far from being neutral, objective structures, bureaucracies are in fact gendered institutions that impose their expectations on the workers within.[20] Given this, bureaucratic structures tend to assume workers will be unencumbered by the external constraints of family, caregiving, and household labor. Presumably, these are tasks that will be fulfilled by a wife so that the worker can meet the organization's demands of time, productivity, and performance.

Since its inception, Acker's theory has been a cornerstone of several studies that assess workers' lived experiences, opportunities, and obstacles within occupations.[21] These studies examine how gendered organizations and occupations affect the organizational culture, promotion patterns, and workplace norms in various jobs.[22] They also provide a basis for conceptualizing some of the challenges tokens can face at work. If occupations are gendered, those who are in the numerical minority should, theoretically, face issues that are structured by the gendered expectations, norms, and implicit responsibilities of these jobs.

Several researchers have built on this premise to consider tokenization when men work in occupations that are considered "female." One of the seminal studies on this subject is Christine Williams's *Still a Man's World*.[23] Dealing with men who work in nontraditional occupations, Williams questions the extent to which their experiences with tokenism mirror Kanter's conclusions.[24] To this end, Williams interviews men employed as nurses, librarians, social workers, and teachers. In each of these occupations, men constitute a numerical minority. Thus, hypothetically, they should encounter tokenized social processes that mirror those of the women who work as traders on Wall Street, are employed as doctors, or work in construction.[25]

In contrast, Williams's findings yield complicated and somewhat surprising results.[26] Rather than experiencing aspects of tokenization like marginalization, invisibility, and presumptions of incompetence, the men in Williams's study are actually welcomed into the professions by their female counterparts. They are perceived by colleagues and customers alike to be *more* competent than women in the same jobs, even when these women have more experience, seniority, or training. They are also more apt to develop close ties with supervisors—often male—thus putting them in line for promotions and upward mobility. These dynamics run counter to what Kanter predicts token males might experience in their work lives and are markedly different from the experiences women have when they are in the minority in male-dominated fields.[27]

Even more interesting, Williams's work shows that for her sample, when men *do* experience tokenization, these processes can actually work in their favor rather than to their detriment.[28] For instance, men in "female" professions *do* encounter the heightened visibility that Kanter describes as characteristic of the token.[29] However, this does not necessarily mean that these men are adversely affected by their conspicuousness. In contrast, their visibility offers them more attention, notice, and interest, which can make them easily identifiable for promotion.

Williams's work thus shows that tokenism works in a very different fashion for men employed in female-dominated fields than it does for women who work mostly among men.[30] In fact, Williams suggests that men in these professions actually experience a "glass escalator" effect that runs counter to the "glass ceiling," which confronts many women who do men's work. The glass ceiling metaphor describes the invisible, felt-but-not-seen obstacle that hinders women's upward mobility. While women in certain jobs may encounter a glass ceiling, Williams contends that for men in women's jobs, tokenization can work to their benefit by putting them on a glass escalator. They are therefore pushed up and out of these female-dominated professions into supervisory, high-prestige positions that are seen as more appropriate for men. Thus, through their heightened visibility, warm reception from women, and close associations with male supervisors, men who are kindergarten teachers, for example, may find themselves fast-tracked into the position of principal or other administrative job. This is an obvious departure from Kanter's theorizing and one that indicates that the social prestige of masculinity plays a role in shaping the token experience.[31]

Jennifer Pierce's work also echoes Williams's conclusions.[32] In her study of gendered occupations in the legal field, Pierce analyzes the gendered performance, emotional labor, and workplace interactions of attorneys, paralegals, and legal secretaries in a large firm.[33] Pierce notes the ways that gender creates differences in each of these areas. She finds that among attorneys, who are predominantly male, certain kinds of workplace emotion and performance are acceptable. Men in these jobs are permitted, even encouraged, to display a "strategic friendliness" in which they are only as genial and convivial as necessary to achieve their objectives. They are also permitted to behave as "Rambo litigators," adopting a belligerent, persistent, and highly aggressive stance in interacting with peers and subordinates.[34] In contrast, women attorneys who attempt to display these characteristics are deemed shrill and unfeminine and typically incur sanctions for what is considered inappropriate behavior.

Pierce finds that the experiences of paralegals and legal secretaries in the firm are a bit different from those of attorneys. Here, most of the employees are female. Consequently, women workers in these areas are expected to engage in mothering, deference, and caretaking in relation to the (mostly male) attorneys. Yet the few men who are employed as paralegals and legal secretaries are not held to these unwritten job rules. They are not attentive to the male lawyers in this way and rarely, if ever, face any penalties for their lack of caregiving. Additionally, like the men in Williams's study, male attorneys often encourage male paralegals to consider becoming lawyers—a higher status, higher prestige position seen as more fitting for men than paralegal or legal secretary work.[35]

Pierce's research highlights how occupations are gendered in ways that have concrete outcomes for the workers involved.[36] The job of a litigator entails the strategic friendliness and Rambo style of interaction that Pierce describes, but women lawyers in this male-dominated occupation are generally not encouraged to deploy these strategies. Conversely, the job of a paralegal involves tacit acts of deference, caretaking, and nurturing, making it a feminized job such that men are implicitly seen as unsuited for this work.

By focusing on the ways occupations are gendered, Pierce's work has implications for understanding how tokenism is shaped by gender.[37] In particular, the male paralegals, like the male nurses, teachers, social workers, and librarians in Williams's research, carry into the occupational expectations the privileges and status associated with being men.[38] When men work in culturally feminized occupations, their higher status means their token experience does not necessarily result in ostracism, isolation, or marginalization. In fact, it can mean additional opportunities for collegial camaraderie, upward mobility, and professional advancement.

The work on tokenism can be seen as a useful framework for assessing those in the minority; however, it should not necessarily be applied as a blanket theory to explain all numerically outnumbered groups. The token experience is influenced by complex issues of power and hegemony that those in the minority bring into the larger group, and these can vary greatly depending on the gendered occupation and a host of other related factors. Furthermore, the "feminine" attributes associated with these gendered occupations help facilitate men's added advantage in these fields. Thus, while women surrounded by male workers may face repeated and severe obstacles to upward mobility, men who are outnumbered by female peers may find that their minority position is dramatically affected by the prestige and status that accompanies masculinity. This can result in extra attention, close ties to colleagues, and a fast track to the upper tiers of the profession.

The research on gendered occupations is thus useful for further developing the token theory. These studies add to the literature by assessing how the cultural status groups bring into the token experience influences the shape, form, and outcomes of tokenization. Yet there is still room for additional research that fleshes out the ways that tokenism works in various contexts. Specifically, these studies tend to show how tokenism perpetuates and maintains gender inequality, even when men are the ones who constitute the numerical minority. But how does the theory of tokenism pertain to other groups who are in the minority in the workplace?

Black Professionals in Predominantly White Workplaces

Black professional workers today inhabit a rather unique sociohistorical location. For most of American history, black professionals made up a tiny fraction of the workforce, and they often serviced predominantly black clientele. Slavery, legal segregation, and other forms of discrimination closed many doors to blacks who may have aspired to professional jobs and often meant the only entrée into the professions was earning a degree from a black university and then limiting oneself to entrepreneurship with or building a client base of other blacks. Historically, then, black professional classes have consisted primarily of relatively small numbers of lawyers, doctors, entrepreneurs, and teachers who served mostly black communities (and saw limited economic returns as a result).

These conditions changed with the advent of the civil rights movement and later with the onset of affirmative action. In the aftermath of the Civil Rights Act of 1964, educational institutions and workplaces were prohibited from discriminating against employees on the basis of race and other factors. This created opportunities for black students to attend predominantly white colleges and universities that had previously denied them entry on the basis of race. This meant that black colleges and universities (which often operated with smaller budgets, endowments, and alumni donations) were no longer their only option for educational training.

Equally significant, beginning in the 1980s, affirmative action policies designed to facilitate diversity in the workplace opened some doors to black professionals as well. This meant that by the 1990s, a class of black professionals existed that looked different from that of previous generations. Unlike their predecessors, these black professionals worked in a variety of fields, had in many cases been trained at elite, predominantly white universities, and were employed in racially integrated settings. Affirmative action policies meant that black workers had access to aspects of the professional world that had been denied to blacks seeking employment in previous generations.

However, it is important to point out that affirmative action policies have hardly been met with unequivocal welcome or support./Though these policies were initially intended to rectify systemic, institutional inequality, they quickly encountered resistance from whites who decried their usefulness, fairness, and potential for success. The 1978 *Regents of the University of California v. Bakke* case was an early legal challenge to affirmative action, in which the Supreme Court ultimately decreed that universities could consider race as one of many factors in admissions but could not establish protected slots for people of color. Other legal challenges have reached the Supreme Court in subsequent years (e.g., *Fullilove v. Klutznick* in 1980 and *Grutter v. Bollinger* in 2003) with resulting decisions severely limiting the ways in which employers, universities, and other educational institutions could attempt to maintain racially diverse populations. Black professionals today, then, have likely benefited in some ways from affirmative action (either as direct beneficiaries or in workplaces where employees of color are more common) but have also faced the backlash against it.

The research on black professionals indicates that the token theory can, to some extent, be applied to explain some of the challenges, difficulties, and obstacles that these workers encounter on the job. Most professions are still predominantly made up of white workers. As such, studies of blacks employed in these occupations must take their minority status into consideration. These racial dynamics often have an impact on the ways black professionals experience various aspects of their work environments, and these dynamics contribute to the tokenism that prevails in white work settings.

Black Professionals and Tokenism

Some researchers have openly used the token hypothesis to attempt to explain the issues black workers face in professional positions. For instance, Pamela Jackson, Peggy Thoits, and Howard Taylor use the token framework to assess the experiences of those they describe as part of the

black elite.[39] These authors contend that members of the highest ranking, highest profile occupations encounter isolation, marginalization,
and stereotyping in their jobs. All these factors adversely affect their job
performance by creating additional work, stress, and hassles. Jackson,
Thoits, and Taylor connect these experiences to the numerical representations of black workers in their chosen professions and find that the
issues these employees encounter exemplify the tokenization that accompanies being underrepresented at work.[40]

Other studies of black professional workers echo Jackson, Thoits,
and Taylor's findings.[41] Examples abound in the literature of the ways
that black professionals encounter various forms of marginalization in
their work environments. In their study of black female workers, Charisse Jones and Kumea Shorter-Gooden offer many examples of women
being marginalized or isolated in professional work settings.[42] They also
provide examples of how black women are made to feel invisible in the
workplace, another process in line with Kanter's theory of tokenization.[43] Additionally, Joe Feagin and Melvin Sikes's study of members of
the black middle class gives voice to many examples that indicate that
blacks face similar dynamics at work.[44] Ultimately, these studies show
time and again that marginalization is a factor black professional workers must address.

Still other studies demonstrate that for black professionals, discrimination is a very real aspect of their work experience. Vincent Roscigno's research on black workers documents numerous cases of the
differential—typically unequal—treatment they face relative to their
white colleagues.[45] He cites numerous cases of black workers who are
denied promotions and jobs despite having more seniority and training than the whites who are offered these positions. These workers are
also fired more frequently and arbitrarily than white workers, leading
Roscigno to conclude that "there remains differential treatment based
on race . . . in the public sector—differential treatment that somehow
defies the protection of formalization and affirmative action policies."[46]
Also, Victoria Kaplan's study of black architects finds that these professionals are less likely than their white colleagues to have access to
opportunities for advancement, promotion, and upward mobility.[47] Often, these workers face overt and covert processes of discrimination in
this profession.

The aforementioned studies emphasize how black professionals encounter challenges in the work environment when it comes to interpersonal interactions with their white colleagues. Still other studies show that structural factors influence the occupational niches where black professionals are likely to be concentrated and do so in ways that can affect their token experience. Though these studies may not overtly explore the concept of tokenization, they highlight the broader structural dynamics that can shape black professionals' work lives and put them in positions where tokenism becomes a significant aspect of their work experience.

Sharon Collins's *Black Corporate Executives* is a key work in this regard.[48] Collins's study shows that black executives are often concentrated in community outreach or diversity services positions in their companies. These tend to be jobs with little potential for growth, development, or overall power within the organizational structure. Perhaps more significantly, Collins demonstrates that these positions may emerge in corporations as a consequence of the social and political pressure to be (or at least appear to be) more diverse. Consequently, these jobs may be less secure than others within the organization because when outside pressure begins to wane, so too may the level of internal support for these positions.

Collins's work focuses on how structural issues can affect black professionals within the private sector, but other studies suggest that the patterns she describes may be characteristic for black workers in the public sector as well. Specifically, Marlese Durr and John Logan's study of black professionals who work for the state of New York yields similar conclusions.[49] Durr and Logan conclude that these employees are likely to be concentrated in "racial submarkets," where they work primarily on issues related to diversity, community outreach, and other projects that involve interacting with minority populations in the state. Like the respondents in Collins's study, these state employees find themselves in occupational niches that offer less job security, stability, and prestige than those experienced by their white colleagues.[50]

These latter two studies are useful because they illustrate the ways structural and institutional dynamics perpetuate tokenism in the black professional environment. Collins as well as Durr and Logan reveal that in both the public and private sectors, as a consequence of public pressure, black professionals tend to be shunted off into occupational niches that render them responsible for interacting with minority communities.[51] However, given the relative lack of prestige and support these positions hold within the organization, black workers in these sectors may be even more likely to face the issues of discrimination, marginalization, and isolation attributed to the tokenized. In short, structural dynamics in the political and social spheres may make it especially likely that black professionals will encounter tokenization within the organization and inside the work environment. These pressures may force them into situations in which their offices, positions, and roles are also tokenized.

As a whole, the research on black professionals shows to some extent how the token hypothesis helps to explain some aspects of these workers' experiences. With the exception of Jackson, Thoits, and Taylor, most of this research does not explicitly use the token theory to assess how and why black workers face challenges in professional occupations.[52] Yet the issues black professional workers describe—social isolation, marginalization, stereotyping—are consistent with those Kanter theorizes affect anyone in the numerical minority.[53]

These studies build on research that considers the ways tokenism fosters gender inequality. This research suggests that aspects of the token experience can perpetuate racial inequality in professional work environments. In other words, if tokenism means that black workers encounter marginalization, stereotyping, and isolation in relation to their white colleagues, then they are less likely to be able to rely on networks, mentoring, and other social processes that aid in upward mobility and occupational ascension.

The literature on gender and tokenism reveals that the process is not necessarily identical across groups. The work of various researchers, as already demonstrated, shows that men who are tokenized do not face the same experiences as women who are in the minority.[54] However, these studies tend to draw conclusions from predominantly white samples and work environments. Thus, what they suggest is that *white* men who are tokens in predominantly *white* female occupations ride a glass escalator rather than hit a glass ceiling. Research that examines black men's experiences in predominantly white female occupations has shown the opposite—that these men do *not* encounter the social processes of the glass escalator in the same way, and are unlikely to encounter the close ties with supervisors, warm reception from female colleagues, and presumptions of higher status that facilitate men's advancement to supervisory positions within the field.[55] Thus, considering the intersections of race and gender offers a means of further fleshing out the extent to which the token hypothesis is useful for understanding the experiences of those in the numerical minority. In the next section, I turn to intersectional theory to address this in more detail.

Intersections of Race and Gender: Implications for Black Professionals

Intersectional theory emphasizes how various social categories (e.g., race, gender, class, sexuality, and nationality) overlap to shape individuals' and groups' social outcomes, lived experiences, and opportunities in various sectors of society. A great deal of the research that relies on intersectional theory focuses on the ways race, gender, and class interact. The literature considers how these overlapping factors affect various groups' labor market outcomes, educational opportunities, social activism, and the like.[56]

One of the most important contributions of intersectional theory has been the attention to how various groups simultaneously experience privilege and disadvantage. Given that people are members of multiple social groups, the same individuals may be simultaneously oppressed and advantaged. Multiracial feminist theorists have made this point in numerous contexts to highlight some of the divisions that occur among women in feminist movements.[57] Among women in the feminist movement, for instance, theorists and researchers have pointed out that white women may be oppressed because of their status as women, but they simultaneously retain privilege because of their racial identity. Failure to recognize and address this privilege relative to other women of color can imperil solidarity across gender lines and the ability to work collectively to improve conditions for all women.[58]

Several studies have employed an intersectional perspective to assess the challenges facing women of color in professional work settings. Most of these analyses build on the research that documents the challenges that minority professionals face. However, the research that focuses on women of color shows that while these women experience challenges that are generally present for minorities in the workplace, their experiences reflect the intersections of race and gender to reveal complexities, issues, and obstacles that would not necessarily be present for all workers. In other words, these studies highlight how professional women of color experience a work environment that is both gendered *and* racialized.

In her recent work, Joan Acker offers an excellent theoretical account of how organizational practices can have particular implications for various workers, including but not limited to minority women. Acker contends that within organizations there exists raced, gendered, and classed practices that she describes as "inequality regimes."[59] These regimes consist of the basic, everyday interactions, structures, and dynamics that maintain various forms of inequality. Thus, the practice of expecting women workers to make and serve coffee or take the minutes in a meeting would be an example of a gendered inequality regime. This has particular implications for women of color, who may be subjected to multiple forms of inequality by virtue of race, gender, and class, leading to occupational hierarchies and disadvantaged positioning within an organization.

Ella Bell and Stella Nkomo offer a piercing empirical assessment of the ways race and gender intersect to create different outcomes for black and white professional women.[60] While Bell and Nkomo identify some similarities for women in professional environments—gendered stereotypes, perceptions about their inability to balance work and family—they also reveal how black women encounter challenges that are clearly racialized as well as gendered.[61] These black professional women face stereotypes about their perceived heightened sexuality, the presumption that they are mean and cold, and the notion that they are less intelligent than their white peers. These divergent experiences not only serve to inhibit solidarity between black and white women but also highlight how race and gender intersect to leave white women free from racial stereotypes about their capabilities, competence, and work ethic, while subjecting black women to racial inequality that complicates the challenges that accompany being female in a corporate environment.

Yanick St. Jean and Joe Feagin's study *Double Burden* reveals similar challenges for black female workers.[62] Drawing on focus groups and intensive interviews with black women discussing a range of subjects, these respondents reveal that they face comparable issues in professional settings. However, St. Jean and Feagin highlight how black women's status in professional work environments can also lead to friction from black male colleagues, who may view black women as taking away "their" jobs. Once again, the intersections of race and gender reveal a more complicated picture of the professional work environment. The perception that black professional women are a threat to black men reflects issues of gender, race, and labor that have historical origins in black men's and women's differential work patterns. This is an issue that is unlikely to be present for white professional women, given that white men are hardly underrepresented in these occupational settings. A focus on intersections of gender and race, however, highlights the fact that black women can face suspicion, stereotypes, and affronts from black men and white women colleagues.

Although, according to intersectional theory, black workers can and do face tokenization, their experiences are not the same across the board. Black women encounter challenges in professional work spaces that clearly reflect the ways gender and race operate together to shape how these women are perceived as well as how they are treated. For them, the token experience does not stop with issues of marginalization, isolation, and stereotyping. Rather, intersections of gender and race shape the specific ways these issues are manifested.

Sociological literature offers several important contributions: theoretical paradigms to assess the work experiences of those who are in the minority, empirical research that verifies that tokenism explains some aspects of black professionals' work lives, and studies that show how the token experience varies depending on the tokens in question. However, some groups are still left out of the research on professional workers. In particular, the research has yet to consider how black men fare in professional settings and how intersections of race and gender shape their experiences with tokenism. We know that the token theory explains some of the occupational challenges facing black professionals, but the literature on black female workers has shown us how this is influenced by gender as well as race.[63] From the work on how the gender of the token influences the token experience, we also know that these men's encounters with tokenism do not necessarily parallel those of black female workers.[64] These studies thus leave us with several unanswered questions: What experiences do black men have in professional work settings? How does tokenization shape the challenges, problems, and opportunities they face? How does their social status as men affect the ways they are tokenized as members of a racial minority group? How do intersections of race and gender inform their occupational experiences?

The Current Study

In this book, I attempt to answer these questions. I place the experiences of black professional men at the center of my analysis to consider the particular issues, challenges, obstacles, and opportunities they face in settings where they are part of a racial minority—but the gendered majority. More specifically, I argue that intersections of race and gender, coupled with work in a male-dominated, gendered occupation, put black men in a position in which the original concept of tokenization fits them imperfectly. In fact, I contend that black professional men in these jobs experience a phenomenon I describe as "partial tokenization."

I argue that partial tokenization reflects both intersecting categories (race, gender, class) and the gendering of occupations. Specifically, I contend that when minority men work in masculinized jobs, they experience partial tokenization because of their ability to conform to the gendered dynamics of the occupation despite their status as a racial minority. This leads them to establish a position whereby they enjoy some of the benefits of being in the majority but are not fully included in the dominant group. In this position, partial tokens do not fully realize all of the aspects of tokenization Kanter describes.[65] Rather, they have a more complicated experience that shapes various aspects of their lives in the occupational arena.

The concept of partial tokenization thus builds on Kanter's original work. Significantly, though, it also moves past her formulation and those of the scholars who have "gendered" the token to emphasize the intersections of race and gender in creating a very specific experience for those in the numerical minority.[66] For the most part, research that considers tokenism tends to focus on either race or gender. These studies generally consider men or women who are tokenized in gendered occupations without paying close attention to race, or they examine how racial minorities are tokenized in predominantly white settings in the absence of an analysis of gender. Studies of black women professionals do address both race and gender but yield very specific results because black women are socially disadvantaged in both areas. The theory of partial tokenism offers an alternative theoretical framework that explicitly takes into consideration the intersections of race and gender as well as the importance of gendered occupations. The theory thus helps explain the rather contradictory experiences some racial minorities can encounter in predominantly white work settings.

To show the experience of partial tokenization, I focus on black men in male-dominated fields. The men who are the subjects of this study are employed as doctors, lawyers, engineers, and bankers. Data were collected through intensive, semistructured interviews. (More information about the research methodology is available in the Appendix.) Each of these fields is male-dominated but contains very low percentages of black men (see Table 1.1). As such, these men are clearly in the racial minority at work, but their gender allows them some access to the dominant group. Focusing on black men in these occupations thus offers an

TABLE 1.1 PERCENTAGES OF MALES EMPLOYED AS DOCTORS, LAWYERS, ENGINEERS, AND BANKERS

	Total (%)	Black (%)	White, Non-Hispanic (%)	Hispanic (%)	Asian, Non-Hispanic (%)	American Indian/ Alaska Native, Non-Hispanic (%)	Hawaiian Native and Pacific Islander, Non-Hispanic (%)
Physicians/ Surgeons*	72.23	1.88	41.66	3.39	7.84	0.09	—
Lawyers[†]	59.24	1.88	51.62	1.99	3.18	0.09	0.07
Engineers[‡]	88.46	2.47	67.47	4.57	12.22	0.19	—
Bankers[§]	56.43	2.93	41.47	2.7	8.84	0.11	0.09

* Data on physicians/surgeons: From American Medical Association, *Physician Characteristics and Distribution in the US* (Chicago: American Medical Association, 2008). Other/unknown males = 17.4 percent.

[†] Data on lawyers: From the 2009 EEO-1 National Aggregate Report (code 54111). The category includes professional-level employees in the offices of lawyers.

[‡] Data on engineers: From National Science Foundation, Division of Science Resources Statistics, Scientists and Engineers Statistical Data System (SESTAT), table 9-7: Employed Scientists and Engineers, by Occupation, Highest Degree Level, Race/Ethnicity, and Sex: 2006.

[§] Data on bankers: From the 2009 EEO-1 National Aggregate Report (codes 52311, 523, 52211). The category includes professional-level commercial, investment, securities, and other financial investment bankers.

ideal way to study how race and gender interact to create the experience of partial tokenization. Additionally, this analysis contributes to the literature and discussion of black professional workers and the black middle class by highlighting how black men encounter occupational challenges and issues that may have been previously overlooked.

In this book, I argue that partial tokenization is manifested in five areas: (1) general challenges, (2) relationships with others in the same numerical minority group, (3) interactions with other numerical minorities, (4) informal roles, and (5) performance of emotional labor. In the subsequent chapters, I highlight how black men experience partial tokenization through each of these occupational phenomena.

2 | The General Experience of Partial Tokenization

What experiences do black men have when they are in the racial minority in male-dominated jobs? In many ways, this is the central question that motivated this research study. What trajectories do black men follow into these occupations? What issues and opportunities accompany the racial dynamics they face?

In some ways, black men's experiences reflect those of other professionals of color in predominantly white work settings.[1] Race remains an issue for them, but they do not necessarily describe it as one that drives every aspect of their occupational lives. However, the professions afford class privileges—material comforts, benefits, and opportunities—of which the men are quite aware. Mitch, a twenty-nine-year-old emergency room doctor, acknowledges, "I never dreamed that I would have the amount of money I make now," but he still concedes that this financial success does not completely alleviate some of the challenges that accompany being a black male doctor.

In this chapter, I consider the men's early interest in and pathways to their occupational fields. I also describe the nature of the relationships they forge and maintain with colleagues, given that these are a critical factor in the token experiences. In so doing, I offer a general context for assessing black men's work in these jobs. Following this, I consider how black men experience partial tokenization in this environment.

General Backgrounds of Black Professional Men

Entering the Field

Most of the men in this study describe an early interest in the career field they selected. Engineers remember being boys who loved to study math and science and figure out how things worked. Doctors talk of being fascinated by medicine in their youth. Thus, many men in the sample are employed in jobs that were a natural fit for their early passions.

That men of any racial group might be interested in science, math, and other such fields is not surprising. Researchers who study gender and work have long argued that gender socialization compels children to cultivate traits and interests that reflect culturally acceptable ideas about femininity and masculinity.[2] These traits can inform the sorts of educational and occupational choices that individuals make later in life. Thus, if girls are taught from a young age that they should be nurturing and caring and that they might enjoy reading and writing, then girls may gravitate toward fields such as early childhood education in their academic and professional career paths. Conversely, when boys are pushed to take an interest in active physical play and science, this can compel them to pursue careers in fields like engineering or sports medicine. Further, these gender divergences can help reinforce inequalities in pay and prestige because male-dominated fields, like engineering and medicine, tend to pay more than female-dominated fields, like teaching.

Jared is a forty-seven-year-old engineering professor. He describes an early curiosity that set him on his current career path:

> My own interest was in physical things. I know that as a child, maybe starting around elementary school, I noticed that I had certain questions that I pondered. I remember wondering if it took the same amount of time for a ball to fall as it did to go up in the air. That was just a question I had. I always liked to spin things—anything. And my father played golf, and one of the things that was a great thing to spin were the little things he used to mark his balls—the spinning tops. So those types of things were always interesting.

As Jared indicates, his questions and curiosity about physics shaped aspects of his early childhood. When he was older, these interests grew into a realization that engineering existed as a plausible career path that would satisfy his passion for the physical sciences. Additionally, Jared offers clues to a class background that may have made a career in engineering seem more easily accessible. Note that he mentions that his father golfs, a sport traditionally associated with the upper middle class. This background may have helped him see ways to translate his interest in engineering into a career.

Mitch, the emergency room doctor, describes a similar pattern of an early focus on his eventual career. His interest in the medical field dates back to his childhood and only grew with time:

> I think my mother always says that—my mother and father said that since I was a kid, I always wanted to be a doctor. I always said I wanted to be a brain surgeon a long time ago, and I guess it was seeing—my parents are very big into black history and making sure that I got my feel of it, but I went to an all-black private school when I was in elementary school, and so we saw a lot of stuff on Charles Drew and things like that, and I think I just got fascinated and never let it go.

Like Jared, Mitch's early appreciation for medicine gave way to a career that allowed him to pursue his interests and goals. Though Mitch references attending a private elementary school, he also describes his background as working class. However, as he states above, his parents took pains to make sure that he had access to educational and social opportunities that would allow him to develop his academic potential as fully as possible. As with Jared, this early exposure to some of the aspects of class privilege (e.g., private school) may have functioned to make a career in a professional occupation appear more easily reachable.

Some respondents trace their interests in their current careers to effective school and academic programs designed to target high-performing students, particularly those who happened to be minorities. George, a forty-nine-year-old engineering professor, describes being positively influenced by just such a program:

So [my interest in] engineering started early. I was in a program in high school called Developing Engineering Students, and it worked. I worked there during summers at the local McDonnell Douglas plant, which has since been acquired by Boeing. . . . But the idea was to give high school students—minority students— exposure to basic engineering principles in things like soldering, drafting, the math, and various sciences (physics, chemistry, and so on) with the intent of persuading those students to . . . be engineering majors in college. Which I did.

Unlike Jared and Mitch, George does not cite an incipient interest in engineering. However, academic programs that target gifted students and seek to introduce them to the field were influential in shaping his subsequent interest in this work.

Still other men describe academic programs that influenced them even later in life. Felton, a banker in his fifties, contends that it was not until college that he was exposed to a class that opened his eyes to the possibility of a career in finance. Felton shares a story of a professor, who, after reading a class assignment, encouraged him to take more economics classes with an eye toward pursuing an MBA:

He said many people have the ability to underwrite and analyze, but you have the ability to communicate that where other people understand. He said that's a gift. He said what I would advise you to do is take some more of those econ classes—economics. Getting into the numbers but not to the extent that accounting does. [That had been] my initial pursuit. He said I can see that in your writing; I can see that in your personality. He said you're not a numbers guy. He said, obviously, there were some little nit-picky errors that were in your writing, but globally, it was fine, but it obviously needs a little work. But he said you're not into the details; you're a big picture person. So from that I looked at econ—economics.

Felton describes the class and encouragement he received from his professor as a critical factor shaping his interest in banking and finance.

For yet other men, their early interest in their careers was guided by family and/or community influences. Some men followed parents' inroads; others knew extended family members or family friends whose experience provided a window into the occupational possibilities of their chosen career path. Kurtis is a forty-four-year-old dermatologist who comes from a veritable family of physicians:

> Well, my dad's a physician. And so I think that probably—obviously, that put it in my head. If your dad's a baseball player, you'd probably play baseball to a degree. But I also came from a community—Los Angeles has the highest number of black physicians in the world, except for, I think, DC was a close second. And so it was great. Every time you looked up, it was just sort of normal to have eleven, twelve guys around the house who were all doctors, so it was not anything special. [My dad's] a gynecologist. My uncle was a radiologist; my other uncle was an anesthesiologist; my aunt's a surgeon; my cousin Cooper is a neurologist. So we have a lot of physicians in our family.

This early exposure to a number of black doctors had a clear impact on Kurtis. He quips: "Realizing it was nothing special, I said, well, maybe I can do this thing. If it just takes perseverance and doesn't take raw intellect, I think I'll be all right." As he alludes, seeing the discipline, hard work, and dedication it takes to become a doctor, coupled with the realization that it is an attainable goal, helped hone his interest in the field.

Another doctor, Lionel, describes a similar experience of being exposed to medical professionals early on in life:

> My grandmother was a nurse, and so I was used to going to the VA hospital in Philadelphia and visiting, and so I became interested in that. I became interested in science along the way as sort of an intellectual pursuit. I knew a lot of African American doctors when I was growing up, so there were a lot of professional people that I was surrounded by. My parents are not physicians, but they are both professionals themselves, and I was surrounded by a lot of folks like that.

While neither of his parents offers the direct example of the doctor's life, Lionel does have the modeling of this occupational path via people in his community and in his parents' social circle. As with Jared and Mitch, growing up with exposure to certain aspects of class privilege— in Lionel's case, community acquaintances and friends who worked in professional occupations—may have helped Lionel see a career in medicine as a realistic, attainable goal.

As the examples of these men have shown, personal interests are often key in pushing black professional men to choose these sorts of male-dominated fields. Whether their early interests were shaped by incipient questions, educational programs, or exposure to others in the field, in many cases, these men pursued the careers they did because these careers reflected their long-held interests, curiosities, and preferences.

Relationships at Work

Once in their respective jobs, black men describe relationships with others as critical to their occupational survival and upward mobility. For lawyers, doctors, bankers, and engineers, being able to develop and maintain positive ties to coworkers, supervisors, and customers was a critical part of the work they did. These relationships helped ensure plum assignments, higher salaries, raises, and promotions. Thus, this social aspect of work is often regarded with the same importance as the technical aspect. Respondent after respondent echoes the assertion made by Lionel, the emergency room doctor, who describes these relationships as "absolutely critical," or by Michael, an engineer, who says that these connections to other coworkers "make or break your success."

Fortunately, most men describe having very strong, positive relationships with their colleagues. In fact, many characterize at least a few colleagues as personal friends with whom they have relationships that transcend the work environment. Nathan, a thirty-five-year-old emergency room doctor, describes his work-related friendships:

> Probably, out of the ten that are in my age group, I'd say seven of them are friends. We hang out. Whether girlfriends or wives or—not too many of them have kids, but we all go out together.

We all go out to dinner and drinks. A couple of us live in the same neighborhoods, so we get together on that aspect as well.

This social dynamic helps Nathan find increased enjoyment in his work life. Friendships with colleagues facilitate a work environment that he describes as generally positive.

Kojo, a sixty-two-year-old lawyer for a major corporation, also describes developing friendships with coworkers:

> [Work friendships develop] over the long haul. For me, it takes a while before I consider a person a friend—and just over the years, through either working directly with each other or getting to know each other generally outside of here. Working together—but also once you get to know someone away from the office and get to know something about them personally, their families, their family situation, their background—that's what helps to solidify and to grow a friendship, in my mind.

Though Kojo considers himself someone who does not make friends easily, he does describe friendships that developed with colleagues over time. As Nathan expresses, this helps to make the work environment a more pleasant place.

Other respondents describe friendships growing from common interests outside of the workplace. Michael, the engineer, gives an example of ties that develop from shared problems at work that led to realizations of mutual interests in other spheres:

> Common interests. We had something in common—normally, common problems with the research and stuff. You know, "I tried so-and-so's method and it doesn't work." "You know, the same thing happened to me." And so that's how a lot of things started. [Our common interests were] football, cars. [Back in] grad school, it was women at the time. So these sort of things. Travel. Things like that.

Here, Michael describes how shared experiences led to the realization of common interests in sports, cars, and—before he got married—women.

Significantly, the mutual interests also reflect the gender dynamics in engineering. As a male-dominated field, it is perhaps not surprising that he and other colleagues bond over stereotypically masculine interests, like athletics, cars, and women.

Overall, men in these jobs describe a work environment that involves collegial relationships, including friendships with coworkers. They may not have the same level and depth of friendships with everyone in the workplace, but the men usually cite a few colleagues whom they consider to be friends rather than associates or acquaintances. As Michael's example shows, these friendships may develop out of discovering interests that are likely to be shared in male-dominated jobs. Or, as in the cases of Nathan and Kojo, they can emerge in a more organic fashion. Ultimately, however, black professional men suggest that their work environments are characterized by the need for solid, dependable relationships and that they are able to establish friendships in this context.

Black men interviewed for this study describe a general sense of satisfaction with their jobs. They enjoy what they do and appreciate the friendships that develop as a result of their work. However, this is not to suggest that their work environments are completely free from problems, issues, and challenges. Though they are in the numerical minority, the obstacles they face are only partly explained by Rosabeth Moss Kanter's token theory.[3] Black professional men encounter partial tokenization in these environments such that the intersections of race and gender mean that some aspects of token theory apply to them, while others fail to capture their experiences.

Heightened Visibility

Among the perceptual tendencies that characterize the token's experience is *heightened visibility*, which leads to increased attention. Tokens are conspicuous because they are fewer in number than the dominant group. As such, they stand out and are easily noticed, particularly when they make a mistake. Being in the minority thus tends to make them the "subject of conversation, questioning, gossip, and careful scrutiny."[4] Consequently, tokens' heightened visibility can result in performance pressures. Because they are so noticeable, tokens are likely to become symbols or representatives of the groups to which they belong. As

Kanter writes, "The women were visible as category members, because of their social type. This loaded all of their acts with extra symbolic consequences and gave them the burden of representing their category, not just themselves."[5] This creates additional pressure for tokens to do excellent work and to avoid any mistakes because they quickly become aware that they might be seen as representatives of their group rather than simply as individuals.

Significantly, Kanter theorizes that this heightened visibility can create negative consequences.[6] She suggests that tokens, in particular, may encounter a fear of visibility. Given the pressure under which tokens operate, Kanter posits, they begin to shun the attention and scrutiny they receive.[7] Even solid, strong performances do not necessarily lead them to welcome attention because of the possibility that male supervisors may be "shown up" by their successes. Therefore, tokens strive to keep a low profile and minimize any attention to avoid making an already precarious situation any more unstable.

There are a number of ways in which the experience of heightened visibility reveals black professional men's partial tokenization in male-dominated work environments. By virtue of their low numbers, black men *do* experience the heightened visibility that accompanies tokenization. However, this is not the entire picture. While some aspects of visibility lead to the adverse consequences that Kanter predicts, the men report other, positive aspects of visibility that they feel operate to their advantage more so than to their detriment.

Downsides of Heightened Visibility

Look Sharp! Dress and Personal Comportment

For many men, the increased attention they draw in the work environment manifests itself in ways that reflect Kanter's arguments.[8] For one thing, the fact that they are so visible means they are always conscious of their bearing and personal appearance. As Kanter writes, "The extension of consequences for those in token statuses may increase their self-consciousness about their self-presentation and about their decisions, and can change the nature of the decisions that get made. Decisions about what to wear and who to sit with at lunch are not casual."[9] Questions about dress and self-presentation are absolutely critical for black male professionals, many of whom are very conscious of their appearance in the workplace.

Woody is a twenty-nine-year-old lawyer in a large firm. While he enjoys practicing law, he has doubts about his ability to be made a partner, given that few blacks have reached this milestone. He describes the importance of always being well dressed at work:

> Why are you wearing a suit? Because I have to wear a suit. You [whites] don't have to wear a suit. You can come in with a polo shirt on, and no one's going to question that you're a lawyer. And forget being a lawyer; no one's going to question that you're supposed to be here. God forbid for me to decide to not wear a tie. You know what I mean? It's jeans day; everyone else can wear jeans. I can't wear jeans.

Earlier in his interview, Woody describes the numerical dynamics in his firm. Black attorneys are but a few, and he is one of only two black male lawyers at the firm's local office. As such, this heightened visibility puts him in a position in which he always feels observed and scrutinized. As a consequence, dressing casually is not an option because he knows that he would be watched, discussed, and potentially taken less seriously.

Warren is another attorney who speaks about the importance of careful self-presentation, particularly when it comes to dress:

> Once you enter the professional world, you got to act professional. And I've always felt that's probably in a higher standard for me—for people of color—to be taken seriously. For example, I wear a suit every day. We don't have a suit policy; this is a business-casual office. But I wear a suit every day. And I always have and probably always will. It's not like once I made partner, I said, well good, now I can take my tie off like everybody else. So you can't [be yourself], but I don't think anybody can be themselves in a professional environment. But because, culturally, my background is so different, I can be less of myself. So, for example, on the weekend, somebody—Joe Blow—may come in here [as] his normal self, not expecting that many people to be

around, and he may have some cut-off khakis and his flip-flops and a T-shirt on. Well, that's something they're kind of used to seeing and that makes them comfortable, and that's fine. I can't come in here in my normal clothes on Saturday, say, maybe my baggy sweat suit, my hat on, and my earrings in my ears. See what I mean? If I did, it's like what in the world is Warren doing, you know? They don't know this person.

Warren's viewpoint is very similar to Woody's. Both men are keenly aware that as one of very few black professional men in the office, they are more visible and therefore face greater scrutiny from colleagues. As such, this creates pressure to maintain a level of professionalism that they hope will allow them to be taken seriously.

Randy, another lawyer, speaks to this issue as well. He works at a smaller firm that is considered less conventional than the larger ones, but even he regards the need to be professionally dressed at all times as imperative:

> I have to be sharp every day. I *have* to be sharp. I can't come in here looking crazy. I can't—I wish I could get away with that white guys' uniform: Dockers, a blue shirt, and some raggedy loafers of some sort. I got to be clean. Granted, I will say it's recognized: "Dang, Randy, you look sharp today." I got to be. I walk in here and I'm not sharp, somebody'll say, "Do me a favor and carry this box downstairs." So I have to stay clean. So I do. (Emphasis in original.)

Randy's statement, like Woody's and Warren's, highlights the importance of dress for black men in these professions. Significantly, Randy points out that there are critical consequences for failing to meet these heightened standards. As he describes, the day he does not dress like a professional will be the day he is mistaken for someone at a lower status.

Other men describe being careful about self-presentation in other ways. Jack, a black lawyer, explains that in addition to his being vigilant about clothing, it is important that he modulate his voice and tone so as not to stand out: "But I notice you need a low voice. You can't really—it depends on the setting—but, generally, you can't take over the room.

Unless it's your job—unless you're the principal and it's your room. I don't really see other white associates having to take care to do that."

For Jack, heightened visibility means not only that he must dress the part but also that he is under scrutiny that extends to his comportment in other areas. He feels that, unlike his white associates, he has to keep a low, even, well-modulated tone when he speaks and that his exaggerated visibility causes exaggerated vigilance of his behavior in this respect.

In yet another case, Larry, a thirty-six-year-old engineer, describes how facial hair matters for black men dealing with enhanced visibility:

> Like before this role right now, I was wearing a full beard. You know [*laughing*], I'm just . . . in a whole different mode. Before it was clean shaven, I think I kept maybe this mustache now. I may have grown a goatee or something like that but never a full beard—you know, never kind of a scruffy look. Previously, I wouldn't have that presentation. In this [previous] role, it tends to be more of a tech role. Everybody [else can] have a beard. We're in silos, [so] you might have somebody who sits right next to you, and you work on something with them, and you'll never talk to them. You send them e-mails or IMs or whatever. It just tends to be a different arena. But like in the marketing role, people are real [talky], and they're touchy-feely, and they want you to come over and this, that, and the other—interact with them and ask you questions. It's more interactive. And so I think appearances matter more.

As Larry explains, in his previous job, which was more technical and involved minimal interactions with coworkers, he felt free to grow the full beard that was more to his liking. But when he migrated to a position that involved more interaction with coworkers and "touchy-feely" colleagues who expected more personal involvement, the heightened visibility he experienced meant coworkers might notice his beard and draw adverse conclusions about his professionalism and capabilities.

Significantly, Larry's example highlights how intersections of race and gender work together to shape the ways heightened visibility is manifested. While personal comportment is undoubtedly a factor for various groups who are tokenized, the issue of facial hair is obviously most salient for men. For black women, heightened visibility may mean they feel pressure to chemically straighten their hair and to avoid jewelry that appears ethnic. Larry's example shows that for black men, the counterpart to this issue may be that visibility compels them to minimize facial hair.

Finally, Mitch, the emergency room doctor, describes a combination of focusing on his self-presentation in terms of appearance as well as in terms of the persona he adopts when interacting with patients. In discussing the importance of appearance, he says:

> It's something you expect as a black person; you expect to have to earn your respect. . . . I'm much younger than most of the physicians anybody sees, and I'm very nontraditional. I mean, I've got six tattoos, and if I don't have my white coat on, which I wear all day at work, my tattoos on my arms are showing, and that's an immediate discredit.

Mitch's statement is reminiscent of accounts from other doctors of color who assert that the white coat functions as a symbol that earns them respect when patients might otherwise doubt their credentials and skills. He argues, as one of very few black male doctors in his workplace (and often the first one his patients have seen), that the increased visibility makes it necessary to don the white coat as a means of acceding to professional standards.

However, wearing the white coat is not Mitch's only response to the enhanced scrutiny he experiences. He is also very strategic about how he is addressed in front of patients:

> In front of patients, I'm Dr. Baldwin, always, to everybody. No matter who it is—my colleagues, the nurses that I work with, nurse practitioners, physicians, residents—I'm Dr. Baldwin. Outside the patient room, I'm Mitch, and I always tell people, don't call me Dr. Baldwin if I see you out or something like that—that's different. But, yeah, I'm definitely—when I walk into a patient's room, I'm very professional: always Mr. and Mrs. So-and-So, even if [the patient says] call me Jim. All right, I'll call you Jim if you tell me to call you Jim, but otherwise,

you're Mr. Smith, and I'm Dr. Baldwin, and that's how we'll communicate.

Thus, in addition to being careful about his dress, Mitch makes clear here that the enhanced visibility he encounters means that he is purposeful about consistently presenting a professional, polished appearance. As one of a handful of black doctors in his workplace, he insists on being referred to by his title and is unfailingly polite to patients, because he knows that slips in this area may result in his being treated differently.

These men's examples show that the increased visibility they experience has an impact on their self-presentation in the work environment. As one of few black male professionals in these settings, they are always aware that they do not have the leniency to dress sloppily or even casually. In some cases, they must also be conscious of matters like facial hair, vocal tones, and basic manners because they know that enhanced scrutiny means colleagues, customers, and supervisors observe various components of their everyday interactions. As such, part of how these men experience partial tokenization is evident in the heightened visibility they experience and the ways it shapes core aspects of their self-presentation.

Graded Harder Than Others

Black men also suggest that the heightened visibility that draws attention to their personal comportment means they are also graded more harshly than others, particularly more so than their white colleagues. Because there are so few of them in the work environment, the increased attention they bear means their mistakes appear more conspicuous as well. As Kanter writes, "[Tokens'] mistakes . . . were known as readily as other information."[10] Thus, in many cases, respondents opined that one of the consequences of their visibility was that they had fewer margins for error than their white male counterparts because any mistakes they made were immediately obvious and carefully scrutinized.

Jack shares his perception that as a black attorney he is allowed very little room for common error:

When it's time for the blame game, I would think that if you are a minority that is not protected, you have a lot less chance of bouncing back. Any attorney—white, black, or other—can slip up and make a mistake in some kind of way that causes some frustration. Let's say it's not necessarily a mistake that breaks the case, but it's something that is a setback, that causes a frustration. If you are a black associate, my impression, as I was alluding to before, [is that] they will never perceive you the same again. You know, [they might say,] "I always thought of him as a weaker attorney" or "I don't perceive him as strong as the other attorneys," whereas the others can bounce back.

Jack asserts that black male attorneys, because of their heightened visibility, face much more scrutiny, in terms of errors, than their white colleagues. A mistake from a black lawyer is seen as evidence that he is less prepared, skilled, and capable than his white counterparts.

Nathan, the emergency room doctor, agrees that as a black male in his profession, he has far less latitude for error:

I don't know if it's a coincidence, but at the hospital that I work at, I've seen a lot of people who are not African American make mistakes and have their little issues, and when I say "mistakes," I'm not talking about medical errors. I'm just saying [they] get into an argument or disagreement with a patient . . . or staff— just little issues like that. Or [they] have some kind of personal issue that affects their job. But I've seen in the past or heard that other people have had similar issues, and they've been resolved internally or quietly, and then when someone else has an issue, all of a sudden it's, "Oh, he doesn't work here anymore." You know, he's not coming back to this facility. He's only going to go to the other facility. And, to be honest, this happened to three black men, an Indian guy, and a Spanish guy. . . . [So] whenever there's an issue with you, you're always like, well, you can't afford to make mistakes. History shows only three people that I know—four or five people that I know—who have stopped working at this facility since I started four years ago have been people of some kind of color, and [with] everybody else, you could be a good doctor, bad doctor, fast doctor, slow doctor, but they're still here. The only people who were asked not to come back were people of some sort of color.

Nathan's claims highlight an important discrepancy. In his observations, the only people pushed out of the hospital were doctors of color, although white doctors also received patient complaints and made mistakes. While Nathan acknowledges that this could be coincidence, the result is that it makes him much more aware of the role he plays within the hospital and contributes to his viewpoint that he has less margin for error than his white colleagues. This drives him to a heightened vigilance about his behavior, interactions with others, and performance as a doctor because the past patterns of dismissal suggest that as a black male, mistakes on his part can easily lead to termination or reassignment.

Larry, the thirty-six-year-old engineer, speaks to this same dynamic. In discussing what he describes as "the politics" of his job, he says:

> There were certain things that—like if you were black, you were going to have to do some work. I mean, there's no way around it. I mean, your white counterpart could screw up, drop stuff, stuff would fall flat on the floor, and directors and VPs and whomever wouldn't know about it. But there was always a path to recovery, you know? But if you were black, your path to recovery was probably severance to get you out of there. So it's almost like consequences were more exaggerated for blacks.

Unlike Nathan, Larry does not describe observations of a pattern in which professionals of color are pushed out of the company more so than their white colleagues. But he does contend that mistakes by white engineers were overlooked or concealed from higher-ups and supervisors, while black engineers were not granted the same kind of leeway. Again, black male professionals are left with the impression that they must perform flawlessly at work.

Welton, a doctor in his fifties, describes a firsthand experience with what he considers to be the smaller margin of error facing black physicians:

> I've been accused of not practicing medicine correctly by a nurse, by a respiratory therapist. . . . And first of all, they would *never* think to say that to a white doctor, but [they would say] he did it different than we're used to. That's a problem. No, that's a

point of education for you [the nurse]; you need to learn, okay. And since the hospital took what [the nurse] did and decided they were going to discipline me because of that, that's when I have to go out and get the lawyers. But see, that's how they get black physicians backed into a corner, because the black physician is not going to try any trouble; they're like, "Okay, I won't do that." No, no, no. [The hospital] didn't follow the rules. The rules say if someone makes a complaint and it's a nondoctor, it goes to the chief medical officer. Then you're supposed to have peer review. That's what happens to white folks when they *kill people*, okay. Not when they just practice. But for the brothers and the sisters, it's [what happens] when they practice. And for the most part, we go through that, and then we want to go somewhere else. That's how they [white administrators] get us out of their place. Because they're not comfortable with us. Therefore, they do these things knowing that when they do it like that— they give them [black doctors] a hard time—then they go away. And that's why most of the black physicians who either are on staff at Peterson or were on staff at Peterson don't go to Peterson. (Emphasis in original.)

Welton provides an emphatic argument that there is less room for black doctors to make mistakes in terms of basic aspects of practice. As he contends, black physicians are subjected to this extended review when lower-status workers (nurses and respiratory therapists) complain or have questions about their performance. But in his experience, for white doctors to go through this level of oversight, it requires the death of a patient. This perception and his personal experience clearly structure his belief that black doctors are graded much more harshly than their white peers.

These men's stories reveal a pattern wherein the heightened visibility produced by their low numbers means not only that they must "look sharp" and present themselves at all times as people who belong in their respective professions but also that any mistakes they make will be immediately observed and held against them. Rosabeth Moss Kanter writes that the token woman also has to "work hard to have her achievements noticed." She explains that "the women had to put in extra effort to make their technical skills known, and said they worked twice as hard to prove their competence."[11] Black professional men's experiences show the flip side of Kanter's analysis—they not only work hard to prove their competence; they do so with the knowledge that they have very little leeway for error, since any failings will be magnified by their heightened visibility.

These processes reflect these men's position as members of the black middle class. Black professionals, male and female alike, cite examples of having to be vigilant about self-presentation to be taken seriously.[12] In that respect, then, these findings are consistent with existing research that highlights how processes of tokenism affect black professionals. The examples cited here, however, show that for black men, there are specific ways that tokenism is also informed by gender. Black men need to "look sharp" not least because if they do not, they risk being mistakenly perceived as dangerous, threatening people—in line with their cultural image as criminals and miscreants.[13] This is a problem that confronts many black professionals but one that is influenced by race and gender in ways that create specific outcomes for black men.

Thus far, I have examined how tokenism creates adverse occupational experiences for black male professionals. Being in the numerical minority means that these men encounter heightened visibility. Consequently, they face heavy pressure to ensure that their personal appearance meets high standards and perceive that they have less margin for error than their white male colleagues. This is largely consistent with Kanter's formulation and with other studies that explore the challenges facing black professionals.[14] However, in other ways, black men contended that being in the numerical minority could work to their advantage, a claim that represents a departure from the findings in the existing literature.

Benefits of Heightened Visibility

In her study, Kanter generally characterizes heightened visibility as something that ultimately works to the token's detriment.[15] However, not all black men describe their low numbers in their professions as something that negatively affects them. In fact, several men assert that by being in the numerical minority, they attract attention that is actually beneficial to them in advancing particular goals.

Teddy, an engineer, speaks about how being one of few black engineers works to his advantage in securing projects:

> I think that's a blessing and a curse. The blessing would be, generally, a lot of [white colleagues] come out of a technology school, and the only black people they knew were playing sports. And then now here you are, so there's sort of a presumption. So you get the look. But then once you show that you are proficient and you do your job well, then I guess the extra visibility is a plus because it's the exceptional Negro phenomenon, right? So [from their perspective, with] all these other [black men], I'm hugging my purse. But you, you're smart, and you can do great things. So it's been a plus in the sense that I've been able to get very competitive salaries because of that—because the visibility has been cool.

Teddy makes a number of interesting points here. As he describes it, visibility helps him because he stands out as someone who defies the stereotypes most of his white colleagues have about black men. He becomes, in his words, an "exceptional Negro"—one who does not evoke fears of criminality or a sense of danger (again, a viewpoint grounded in gendered racist assumptions about black masculinity). And because he is seen as the rare, talented, safe black man, he becomes a valuable commodity and can thus command a decent salary. The contradiction here, however, is that his colleagues' view still reinforces the general idea that blacks, at large, are associated with substandard performance, competence, and skills. As Teddy astutely points out, although visibility helps him secure a comfortable salary, it still stems from racialized representations that denigrate black Americans.

Michael, the engineer discussed previously, unambiguously characterizes the heightened visibility he experiences as a positive factor:

> Everyone remembers my name. Everybody knows who I am. And I only have to show up once and say a word, and everybody knows who I am. So while some people would say, "Well, that draws a lot of attention," I would say that's a good thing. You know, use what you've got. So that's a good thing. People see my

name on a paper, they know who I am. [For others], they're kind of like which grad student was that? Or which professor was that? Yeah, I mean, you stand out instantly.

While Teddy casts his visibility as something that has benefits but is grounded in negative stereotypes, Michael views his conspicuousness as something that enables him to highlight his skills and talents. Because he is so visible as one of few black men in engineering, his accomplishments and professional successes reach a wide audience because of his immediate name recognition.

Maxwell, a thirty-four-year-old plastic surgeon, also talks about how visibility can work to his advantage:

It has definitely helped with the other black physicians just because there are only eight black plastic surgeons in [this city]. They were all pretty much spread out. So for patients who have expressed an interest in a black plastic surgeon, it has been a huge help to them because there aren't any others near here. Here, everybody knows who I am. I mean everybody knows who I am because there aren't any other black plastic surgeons around here. So at this hospital, all the hospital staff knows Dr. Graham.

While Maxwell notes that visibility helps him attract a certain share of the available market, it is important that he acknowledges the role demographics play in this. Given the very low number of black plastic surgeons in his metropolitan area, he is, literally, the only black plastic surgeon for miles. Additionally, given the fact that he works on the outskirts of a city with a significant black middle class, these factors coincide to make his visibility a positive rather than a negative.

The descriptions of visibility as something beneficial are more akin to the accounts of white men in female-dominated jobs, who argue that being in the numerical minority leads to more opportunities than are often available to their women colleagues. Rather than feeling constrained, these men feel buoyed by their visibility. White men in the minority in "women's" jobs find that greater visibility makes their accomplishments more obvious and gives them access to opportunities that can further raise their profiles in their fields.[16] Black men share some of the more positive aspects of being in the numerical minority with their white counterparts, whose racial and gender status gives them automatic access to the upside of tokenism.

However, there are key differences present as well. For black professional men, visibility not only helps them gain professional advantages; it also offers benefits that come in the form of social support. In particular, several men talked about how the visibility of being in the numerical minority meant that they received positive attention from other blacks, typically those they encountered as clients or customers. In other words, their visibility attracted not only notice from whites but warm regard from blacks as well.

Mitch, the emergency room doctor, provides a description of feeling touched by the positive response he gets from black patients:

Oftentimes [black patients] who see you in your role will just out of nowhere just tell you how proud of you or how happy they are to see you doing what you're doing. And that's something that's really amazing. You know, when I see people or I see a patient and they say, "Well, I'm calling my daughter and telling her to come up here because this is just amazing. You just make me so proud." Things like that. And then it's something that other people don't get, and it's really nice to have. And then you realize that you are not necessarily an inspiration but more of a light to people. They see that in our community there are young black men out there that are doing good things. I think when people go into an emergency department, they're not expecting you to walk into the room, and you're going to get one [response] or the other. And when they do see you and they do realize you're just a regular person but that you basically endured a lot of struggle in a major way, some people are just overjoyed. Literally *overjoyed* is probably the best word I could find to use. A lot of people say, "I can't believe that you're here and you can take care of me. I can have a black doctor; that's so nice to have now and then." I appreciate that, and that makes me happy.

In this conversation, Mitch asserts another positive dynamic of the heightened visibility he experiences at work. As he suggests, patients rarely expect to be treated by a black male physician; consequently, their reactions will be "one [response] or the other"—they will either be pleasantly surprised or react negatively. However, when black patients react joyfully to seeing him as their doctor, he regards it as one of the best aspects of the visibility that accompanies being one of the few. This has particular relevance given the widespread perpetuation of images of black men as criminals, degenerates, and general drains on society.

Another respondent describes a similar pattern. Warren, the lawyer quoted previously, who is a partner in his law firm, talks about the sense of importance other blacks at the office attached to his promotion:

> When other [black] folks worked here—even on the staff, where we have a lot of people of color—it was very important to them that I made partner. They kind of saw that as an achievement that everybody could share in. So there's an impact on other people of color, especially in my department. When I made partner, there hadn't been a partner made in thirteen years. And so that was even more significant. It was kind of like finally somebody broke through, and, by the way, it was a black man too. And that was a sense of pride.

As with Mitch, it matters to Warren that other blacks are able to view his ascension positively. This is another benefit of heightened visibility. It offers black men the opportunity enjoy the pride others take in their accomplishments. Like Mitch, Warren points out that this is especially significant for black men, who are often represented as largely failing to succeed on occupational, educational, and economic fronts.

Again, the means by which black men feel they benefit from heightened visibility also have implications for our understanding of black professionals' occupational experiences. Much of the literature argues that when black professional workers stand out from their white colleagues, it is to their detriment and usually precedes or is linked to discriminatory treatment.[17] Respondents quoted here, however, interpret heightened visibility as something that operates to their advantage, whether it is through showcasing their high-quality work or by enjoying social support from other blacks who appreciate what they do and how they offer positive images of black masculinity. I do not argue that heightened visibility is uniformly a good thing for black workers; indeed, respondents themselves identify the negative components of the conspicuousness associated with being in the numerical minority. However, the comments quoted here suggest that respondents can find some positive aspects to the visibility they encounter as one of few black male workers in male-dominated occupations.

Summary

For black professional men, their male-dominated work environments are complicated places. They hold jobs they have aspired to for many years, and their choice of profession often stems from a childhood interest. They have been able to develop genuine friendships with some of their colleagues. However, this does not mean that these jobs are devoid of problems or difficulties. Black men certainly encounter challenges and obstacles in these professions. Significantly, though, the issues they face do not precisely fit the token hypothesis. Black men's experiences are better characterized as examples of partial tokenization, and these experiences reflect how gender and race intersect for this minority.

In key ways, black men's experiences in white male-dominated jobs reflect some aspects of tokenism. For instance, their low numbers mean that they stand out among colleagues, leading to the heightened visibility that Rosabeth Moss Kanter describes.[18] This heightened visibility creates a paradigm in which black men encounter great pressure to look and appear "professional" at all times. It also quickly makes them aware that they have marginal room for error—that they will be judged more harshly than the white males who constitute the dominant group in their professions.

Here, race and gender influence the particular ways black professional men negatively experience heightened visibility. Failure to "look sharp" and conform to racialized, gendered depictions of professionalism may mean they are viewed according to racialized, gendered stereotypes of black masculinity. In other words, these men must wear suits, use low voices, and insist on using their official titles to meet (and, often, exceed) standards of professionalism. They cannot, for example, show tattoos or wear hooded sweatshirts, because they then run the risk of being perceived as black men who could potentially be dangerous.

They must create an image of professionalism often associated with white men or suffer stereotyping.

In other ways, however, heightened visibility reveals a more ambiguous picture of how black men are affected by their minority status. Some black men do not experience the "fear of visibility" Kanter attributes to those in the token position.[19] As Kanter describes it, the social and symbolic pressures of visibility cause tokens to strive for invisibility—they seek to blend into the background, avoid opportunities to showcase their successes, and keep a low profile.[20] In contrast, the black professional men I spoke to identify how heightened visibility works to their advantage by allowing them to access occupational rewards, like higher salaries, professional recognition, and an increased customer base. It also offers them the benefit of social and cultural support. Intersections of race, class, and gender also play a role here, in that the relative rarity of black professional men means that respondents are especially likely to enjoy support and even adulation from black customers, patients, or staff. Thus, they do not strive to fade into the background but actively take advantage of the ways that visibility can benefit them. Consequently, these men experience a partial tokenization—even as they struggle with the adverse implications of being highly visible, they still cite advantages that accompany this phenomenon.

Partial tokenization shows us that for these individuals, their experiences as members of the black middle class are somewhat nuanced. Being in the numerical minority does not create a uniformly negative experience in which visibility leads only to challenges. Rather, partial tokenism helps to alleviate some of the obstacles that accompany membership in the black middle class. Men in these jobs, then, may not experience the rage attributed to members of this group who find themselves overwhelmingly marginalized, ignored, and overlooked in these jobs.[21] Instead, they are more prone to a sense of optimism about their career prospects and occupational opportunities that journalist Ellis Cose argues is now more characteristic of some members of the black middle class.[22] This research suggests that our analyses of the black professional class may also need to consider the occupations in which black workers are employed and the extent to which tokenization (or, if applicable, partial tokenization) can mediate some of the issues associated with their positions.

3 | Interacting with Women in the Workplace

L ike black men, women doctors, lawyers, engineers, and bankers are employed in male-dominated fields where they are in the minority. In keeping with their minority status, women make up a relatively small percentage of the workforce in most of these positions (see Table 3.1). This is changing with the legal and medical professions, as, increasingly, women are outpacing men as graduates of legal and medical schools and will soon become the majority of those practicing in these fields. For the time being, however, both women and black men are tokenized in the professional workplace, albeit in different ways and for different reasons. How then do these two groups in the numerical minority interact with each other? More particularly, how do black men interact with others who are in the minority because of gender and not race?

Gender Interactions

There is very little research that explores the nature, scope, and development of black men's relationships with women in the workplace. Some studies that address race and gender more broadly do touch briefly on this topic. When they do, typically the focus is on the connections between black men and black women. In some cases, these studies find

TABLE 3.1 PERCENTAGES OF FEMALES EMPLOYED AS DOCTORS, LAWYERS, ENGINEERS, AND BANKERS

	Total (%)	Black (%)	White, Non-Hispanic (%)	Hispanic (%)	Asian, Non-Hispanic (%)	American Indian/ Alaska Native, Non-Hispanic (%)	Hawaiian Native and Pacific Islander, Non-Hispanic (%)
Physicians/ Surgeons*	27.77	1.64	14.2	1.63	4.5	0.07	—
Lawyers†	40.76	2.8	31.93	1.88	3.52	0.09	0.07
Engineers‡	11.54	0.68	7.41	0.86	2.22	0.06	—
Bankers§	43.56	4.58	30.01	2.65	5.87	0.12	0.07

* Data on physicians/surgeons: From American Medical Association, *Physician Characteristics and Distribution in the U.S.* (Chicago: American Medical Association, 2008). Other/unknown females = 5.79 percent.

† Data on lawyers: From the 2009 EEO-1 National Aggregate Report (code 54111). The category includes professional-level employees in the offices of lawyers.

‡ Data on engineers: From the National Science Foundation, Division of Science Resources Statistics, Scientists and Engineers Statistical Data System (SESTAT), table 9-7: Employed Scientists and Engineers, by Occupation, Highest Degree Level, Race/Ethnicity, and Sex: 2006.

§ Data on bankers: From the 2009 EEO-1 National Aggregate Report (codes 523, 52211, 52311). The category includes professional-level commercial, investment, securities, and other financial investment bankers.

tensions between black women and men over the stereotypes and suggestions that black women are "taking jobs" from black men. In their study of the ways racism and sexism intersect to affect black women, Yanick St. Jean and Joe Feagin cite a focus group respondent who states: "I had been faced with black men, when I first started working, telling me to give up my job for black men, and I was quite angry about that. I don't think I should give up my job."[1] More broadly, sociologist Patricia Hill Collins theorizes that the controlling image of the "educated bitch"—a depiction of assertive, career-driven black women—serves to heighten friction between black men and women over black women's presence in white-collar, professional positions. As Collins writes, "These representations also are used to explain why so many African American women fail to find committed black male partners—they allegedly work too hard, do not know how to support black men, and/or have character traits that make them unappealing to middle-class black men."[2]

These representations paint a picture of conflict between black men and black women, particularly over the issue of work and employment.

To some extent, this conflict is grounded in actual occupational patterns among black workers. Historically, black women were more likely to maintain regular employment than black men, although black men who worked earned higher wages than their female counterparts.[3] Black women currently outpace black men in higher education and are making greater inroads into professional occupations (though black men still constitute a higher percentage of those in professional/managerial jobs).[4] Thus, in the sense that black women are advancing into professional jobs more rapidly than are black men, this can potentially give rise to friction as black women may appear to be usurping stable, white-collar jobs that have traditionally been the province of men. Given that employment is often linked to masculinity, black women's more consistent employment relative to black men can be—and is—construed by some as taking black men's rightful place as wage earners.[5]

Few studies explicitly consider black men's interactions with white women in professional work settings. In this case, there are still historical gendered and racial patterns that could influence how black men interact with white women. Dating from the postslavery era, black men have been cast as sexual predators who specifically seek out white women. Inasmuch as white women have historically—and continue to be—idealized as the epitome of beauty and femininity, this construction serves to promote the argument that they are a natural target for black men's heightened sexuality. This imagery has been used to justify violent means of repression (including lynching), segregation, and other restrictive measures ostensibly intended to protect white women from black men's sexual advances.[6]

Given this history, we can theorize that these racial and gender prejudices could potentially affect the ways black men interact with white women at work. In my previous research on black male nurses, respondents in this predominantly white female field indicate that they are mindful of and seek to avoid language or behaviors that might evoke this image of the black male predator in the eyes of their white female colleagues.[7] Even in male-dominated fields in which white women are less well represented than they are in nursing, this cultural image of black masculinity can still be hypothesized to affect interactions between black men and white women.

Ultimately, existing research leaves much unanswered in terms of black men's professional relationships with women in male-dominated jobs. We know that historical patterns can influence the ways in which black professional men interact with both black and white women at work, but little empirical research examines this specifically. I turn now to Rosabeth Moss Kanter's work to provide more theoretical leverage for analyzing these workplace relationships.[8]

Contrasts: A Way of Interacting with Women

Kanter offers an analysis of how tokens are treated by those in the dominant group and how this treatment serves to influence the ways they interact with others who are also in the minority.[9] She contends that when tokens are present, a constant part of social interaction involves a process she describes as "contrast." This term describes efforts from the dominant group to reinforce their status, normalcy, and centrality within the organization. As Kanter writes:

> The presence of a token or two makes dominants more aware of what they have in common at the same time that it threatens that commonality. . . . The "threat" a token poses is twofold. First, the token represents the danger of challenge to the dominants' premises, either through explicit confrontation by the token or by a disaffected dominant who, through increased awareness, sees the culture for what it is and sees the possibility of alternatives. Second, the self-consciousness created by the token's presence is uncomfortable for people who prefer to operate in casual, superficial, and easygoing ways, without much psychological self-awareness and without the strain of reviewing habitual modes of action—a characteristic stance in the corporate environment.[10]

Ultimately, the presence of those in the numerical minority reminds the members of the dominant group of how their practices and behaviors exclude certain others.

Establishing contrast, then, is a common response to this discomfort. To do this, dominant groups will highlight the differences, real or perceived, between themselves and the tokens. In emphasizing differences between the token and the dominant group, dominants may engage in several strategies. One involves quarantining the token. In this case, dominants may simply work to exclude tokens from occasions, meetings, and networking events. As Kanter describes, members of the dominant group may feel that they cannot fully trust the tokens or that they cannot be completely relaxed and at ease in their presence. Thus, tokens can be quarantined to the extent that they are isolated or completely left out of important social interactions. This can work to the tokens' disadvantage, especially if they are kept from meetings in which they might obtain useful information. Dominants are driven by a desire to retain, in the language of social psychologist Erving Goffman, a backstage where they do not feel the need to monitor themselves in front of those who are seen to be different.[11]

Kanter also argues that establishing contrast leads dominants to put tokens in a position of having to prove their loyalty to the dominant group.[12] She refers to these as "loyalty tests," wherein "the group sought reassurance that the tokens would not turn against the dominants or use any of the information gained through their viewing of the dominants' world to do harm to the group."[13] In imposing these tests, dominant groups expect tokens to show that they can fit in with the larger group and disavow ties to their own. Through this process, tokens show that they are not overly connected to their own group and that they can conform to the cultural and social dictates dominants have established.

In keeping with the need to prove their loyalty to the dominant group, tokens are expected to turn against one another. As Kanter writes, "Assurance could be gained by asking tokens to join with or identify with the dominants against those who represented competing loyalties; in short, dominants pressured tokens to turn against members of their own category."[14] Showing too much connection or solidarity with other tokens highlights tokens' differences from the dominant group (often in a way the dominant group perceives negatively). It can also minimize tokens' capacity to form necessary ties to members of the dominant group. Consequently, in an effort to prove their loyalty, tokens may endorse derogatory remarks about members of their own group or refuse to defend themselves when such comments are made.

In each of these cases, the dominant group's efforts to highlight differences between tokens and themselves shapes how tokens interact with one another. As dominants attempt to reinforce the boundaries between themselves and those in the minority, tokens are isolated and therefore pushed to prove their loyalty to the dominant group's social and cultural mores. As Kanter theorizes, they are then ultimately compelled to turn on one another to show that they can fit in with the larger group.[15]

Kanter's arguments offer a useful theoretical framework for assessing how tokens may interact with one another.[16] However, because she focuses only on women tokens in a male-dominated setting, there is little attention to the ways other groups in the minority may interact with one another. In other words, Kanter examines how the dominant group's efforts to maintain boundaries create fragile relationships among those in the numerical minority.[17] But what happens when there are several groups in the minority?

Very recently, some studies have addressed aspects of this question. Kris Paap's ethnographic study of the ways in which white male construction workers establish racial and gendered boundaries in this occupation addresses interactions between white women and black men, both of whom are in the minority in this field.[18] Paap finds that the black men with whom she worked on construction sites were indifferent, if not outright cool, toward her. Significantly, she notes that as white working-class men attempt to preserve a sense of ownership and control over the construction site, workers who are different by virtue of race and gender are excluded. As such, one of the consequences she observes is that black men, who presumably also feel like outsiders, are reluctant to form ties with white women like her, who are also excluded from the dominant group.

Though she does not explicitly use the token framework, Paap describes a number of cases that reflect just the type of contrasting that Kanter describes. As a woman working construction, Paap is continually reminded of how her body makes her different from the predominantly male workforce on job sites. She also notes that racial stereotypes and generalizations are used to draw attention to black male workers and thus contrast their presence and behaviors with the aggressive, risk-taking forms of (white) masculinity that are prized on the job. Paap argues that contrasting relegates black men to outsiders and makes them uncomfortable with forming ties with white women on the construction site for fear that this will further exacerbate black men's token status.

Her work thus offers some confirmation of Kanter's theories and suggests that in this space, members of different minority groups may have a hard time forming solidarity.

Catherine Turco has also explored the dynamics of black male–white female relationships in a white male–dominated occupation.[19] In her study of the leveraged buyout industry, Turco examines black men and white women to assess the impact of tokenization on these two different groups.[20] She finds that black men perceive that women face greater challenges in this field than they do, and consequently, she argues that black men in the minority are more apt to be empathetic to their plight. These results differ from Paap's findings and Kanter's theorizing in that black professional men are sympathetic to other groups that experience tokenization. This is clearly an important finding but one that still leaves room for additional analysis. Is the leveraged buyout industry unique, or do black men's experiences here extend to other occupations? If black men perceive that women experience more discrimination and difficulty than they do in male-dominated jobs, do these men then seek to achieve solidarity with those in the dominant male group by turning against women workers? If Turco's findings extend to other male-dominated fields and black men are sympathetic to the challenges their women colleagues face, does that affect their behavior and actions in these jobs in any way? How do race and gender intersect to inform the ways black men interact with women of all races in the workplace?

I contend that because these men encounter partial tokenization, they are less likely to engage in the distancing processes Kanter describes among those in the minority.[21] Rather, their interactions with women are more complicated: For some men, intersections of race and gender give them a more precise understanding of how inequality operates through institutional and individual processes, and they are particularly attuned to the ways this affects women as other minorities in the workplace. Additionally, their work in male-dominated occupations sometimes gives black men the gender advantage, which allows them to create fairer work environments for women colleagues. Yet other men endorse dominant ideologies about women (e.g., their unfitness for certain work) and claim that intersections of race and gender actually increase women's opportunities in these jobs, giving them the advantage over black men. Still other black men use the concept of the quarantine to shape their interactions with white women.

It is important that I disclose the possibility that interviewer-interviewee dynamics affected what respondents were willing to share with me. Because I am a woman who was asking male respondents about their interactions with women at work, these men may not have been entirely forthcoming, shaping their answers so as to appear more politically correct than they really are. However, as Christine Williams has noted in her interviews with men in traditionally female jobs, one of the benefits of the intensive interview format is that it allows respondents the latitude and space to construct answers carefully.[22] Thus, while respondents may have couched their language in some cases, I have every reason to believe that their responses honestly reflect their opinions and beliefs about their work experiences.

Showing Loyalty to Women

Tokenization theory predicts that those in the numerical minority must show loyalty to those in the dominant group. Were black men to follow this path, they might emphasize how, specifically, they fit into the male-dominated, often hypermasculine environments that characterize their work settings. This would enable black men to play up how they resemble the members of the dominant group and to join white men in highlighting the differences between men in the organization and the women who are in the numerical minority in most offices.

Many respondents are aware that their work environments are male-dominated spaces. They talk openly about how their jobs and even their industries, more broadly, are places that are probably much more comfortable for men than they are for women. Felton, the banker in his fifties, speaks to the challenges women face in banking:

> I mean, it's tough from a woman's perspective because it's a male-dominated business. Very few women are necessarily looked at as peers, and then the family piece kicks in. You know: Are you going to have a career? Are you going to have family? And those women that choose not necessarily to take the family route first—there are all kind of negative connotations that are

given to them in terms of [whether] they're going to be career oriented. Just the whole dynamics is different.

As Felton notes, the male-dominated nature of the financial industry can be especially tough for women. He first remarks that women are rarely seen immediately as peers and that their (perceived) family responsibilities work against them. The male-dominated industry of banking is thus one that sees women as outsiders and assumes that family obligations will interfere with their work.

Peter, an orthopedic surgeon, remarks on the fact that his medical subspecialty in particular remains one that is geared mostly toward men: "Obviously, it's worse for females in orthopedics. Orthopedics is a very macho field. It used to be [for people going through training] and probably still is. And so even in training, you had to really—basically, you had to always suck it up. You have to learn."

Like Felton, Peter remarks that during his training, he observed orthopedics to be a male-dominated field that, while difficult for everyone, was particularly unkind to women.

Other respondents argue that in these masculinized occupations, black women face particular difficulties because of the intersections of race and gender. Jack, the attorney who dresses carefully and modulates his voice, has this to say:

> I would think that an African American woman is facing far more of a challenge than an African American male. Not only does she deal with the burden of being black and being perceived as not as qualified as these other people. In this profession, let's say, for example, in court, unless the judge is a woman—and you'll probably see my own stereotypes that are coming up—the comments that are associated with women are that they're not as strong, [that] you could probably trust a man with legal issues and not a woman, especially when it comes to weaving together these complex legal issues. I just think [women] have to fight beyond that.

Here, Jack identifies the ways that race and gender intersect to work to black women attorneys' disadvantage. As he explains, not only are women generally perceived as less-competent lawyers; they are seen as even less well qualified if they are black. Jack echoes the conclusions of other sociological studies that point to how the intersections of race and gender create specialized obstacles for black professional women.[23] These statements also reflect Turco's finding that black men are cognizant of ways that the male-dominated culture of their occupations has particular consequences for women.[24]

Despite these men's awareness that they are working in male-dominated industries, they rarely speak of exploiting their gender advantage to ingratiate themselves to members of the dominant group and heighten further the boundaries between themselves and their women colleagues. In other words, men do not show their loyalty to white men by emphasizing gender solidarity at the expense of their female coworkers of any race. Instead, they are much more likely to discuss how they identify with women in their fields and to express solidarity with them.

Maxwell, the thirty-four-year-old plastic surgeon, talks about feeling a sense of identification with women in the medical field, given the challenges they experience:

> I think being a black male, I understand a lot about what they are going through. A lot of women [doctors] will complain that when they walk into the room, patients say, "I have to hang up the phone now because my nurse is in the room." [Women colleagues] used to say that to me all the time. But I would tell them that I would much rather be a nurse than an orderly or an X-ray tech. So I can understand a lot of the stuff that they went through.

Here, Maxwell makes an interesting parallel between his experience and those of his women colleagues, and he argues that the overlap enables him to empathize with the challenges they face. He implies that like them, he faces the issue of what Kanter describes as mistaken identity, wherein those in the minority are immediately associated with whatever position is assumed to best fit their status.[25] Hence, women are mistaken for nurses and black men for orderlies or X-ray technicians. But as Maxwell points out, this experience of being mistaken for someone of lower status enables him to empathize with women in his field.

Ronald, a civil engineering professor, also talks about understanding the challenges women face:

> I think being a black man, I'm very [cognizant] of challenges that women face. Especially in a place like this where they are in the minority. In some ways, I'm less of a minority than they are. And so I think it does [affect how I interact with my women coworkers]. I mean, I certainly think it does. I really understand the things they are going through and am much more sensitive than probably the majority of my colleagues are. It does make me more sympathetic to what women go through. And very much more sensitive, and I try to be understanding.

Like Maxwell, Ronald identifies connections between his experience as a black male and contends that this makes him more sensitive to the challenges women face. In particular, he perceives that he is likely more aware of these issues than most of the white men who constitute the majority of his colleagues. In both cases, then, rather than showing loyalty to white men who are the dominant group, black men talk about being able to understand and empathize with women, who make up another numerical minority group in the workplace.

For several men, this awareness that women face challenges not unlike their own actually leads them to engage in actions designed to ameliorate or at least minimize the problems women encounter. Recognizing that being men in male-dominated fields affords them a level of acceptance, some black men make concerted efforts to legitimize and support their female colleagues. They often do this based on their sense that women in their professions "have it harder" than they do, but they also speak of being motivated to do this out of the recognition that women's challenges mirror their own.

Jared, the forty-seven-year-old engineering professor, speaks to this. He explains that while he has had female students outperform male students on several occasions, the gender dynamics of engineering can still present challenges for women that he tries to address:

> It could be a difficult thing to negotiate; I can see that. Having said that, one of the things that I've tried to do is sometimes do

little things that would tend to make women feel more included. Like when I write a scenario that involves somebody, I will often make that somebody female. So I say, "Suppose a bike rider wants to stop her bike in the quickest time possible or whatever, what should she do?" So, it's a little thing, but it does sort of change the expectations. Or one of the things I know I've said is "This exam will really separate—" instead of saying "the men from the boys," I'll say, "the women from the girls." So even though it's eight or ten women and forty males, why not say it? There's no great campaign that I have, but there's certain things [I do] because I just can appreciate that part of the game is to feel like you're a part of the equation. And if you feel like you're a part of the equation, and you feel like you belong, then that tends to bring out your best performance. But if you always feel like students don't really accept [you], [that] they feel like [you] shouldn't be here, [that you] have [your] own self-doubts, well, then you can sort of shrivel away. But then if there are things that sort of affirm the fact that, yeah, you should be here, we expect you to do well, why not?

Here, Jared explains how he draws from his own experience to empathize with the challenges women may face in the minority, and he describes the concrete steps he takes to try to make women more accepted into the mainstream and the culture of engineering. His example of stating that exams will separate "the women from the girls" in a class mostly made up of male engineering students is particularly significant. Given the overwhelming percentage of men in engineering (85 percent) and the frequency with which male nouns and pronouns are used, making women the normative group in this setting is an especially important way of challenging implicit male biases in the field.

Greg, a lawyer, also talks about recognizing the greater challenges women encounter in the field and attempting to work on their behalf:

Certainly, in the private practice women have it tougher. Women of color have it tougher than that. I'm active; you found me through the Georgia Association for Black Women in Law. I'm on the foundation board. I think that, personally, I have always gotten along with everyone. Certainly, I recognize that we are all in the same boat.

For Greg, the recognition that "we're all in the same boat" means that he sees the importance of joining an organization designed to provide support to black women attorneys given the challenges he sees them facing in the legal field.

Another attorney, Andy, is a partner in a firm. He talks about actively taking steps to promote women, providing them with opportunities for advancement that otherwise might not be forthcoming:

> I sympathize because I understand the issue. And I can look at the numbers and tell that women aren't being as successful as white men. So there's a solidarity in the sense that if there were two people similarly situated with [the] same credentials, [and] both could offer me the same things in a project, I would pick the woman just because, inherently, in my mind, I'm thinking if I don't do it, things aren't going to change. So I would pick the woman.

Here, Andy essentially describes employing affirmative action to select law associates to work on projects. Given that Andy is a partner in his firm, this type of support from someone in his position would be enormously valuable to a junior associate. Thus, his awareness of the challenges women can face in this highly male-dominated field creates a sense of solidarity rather than tension or distance.

In another case, Larry, the thirty-six-year-old engineer, talks about consciously working to eradicate the stereotypes of women that abound in his profession:

> I think women are, especially in a technical area, . . . thought of as airheads—not really knowing what they are talking about or driven by emotions. You know [*in a mocking tone*], "Don't make so-and-so mad." So they're [seen as] more shrouded in emotions, and they're not really capable of thinking rationally enough to diagnose a problem, . . . [and] I can feel their pain. And this is [not just] black women [but] also white women. I'll

talk more with them. Some people will just start shunning them, or something goes on and you see people like [*making a skeptical face*]. Say, if something's wrong with the system, and Jane says, "I think there are duplicate files in the directory," or something. And people [say] little smart comments. So I can feel that. It speaks to—it's a form of disrespect, but it has more to do with the fact that they're female. So maybe I'll say, "Here's what I think it is." And then I'll say something that I know makes no sense, and they're looking at me like what is he talking about, and then she can recover and say, "No I tried that." But that helps her build some sort of credibility.

Here, Larry describes the perceptions women encounter in this male-dominated field, as well as his strategy for helping them offset that. Unlike Andy, he is not in a position to actively advance women through the ranks. But he does take advantage of opportunities to help women be taken more seriously, particularly since he observes a culture in which they are regularly belittled and marginalized.

Weston, a cardiologist, also talks about using his position as a means of modeling better treatment for women. In response to a question about how he feels women of different races experience the medical field relative to black men, he says:

There is *absolutely* more gender bias than racial. This is an environment where it's mostly male, and people say things. There are so many issues of bias—it's considered part of the club, and men enter because of different credentials. I'm a man; I'm in the gentlemen's club. (Emphasis in original.)

When I asked Weston if this perception affected how he treated women with whom he interacted at work, he replied emphatically:

This absolutely *does* impact how I treat women. I give them all respect. Knowing what this world and this country was built upon, I go out of my way to—I have this insatiable drive for excellence and not to be beat. I can't quit. I have an all-out war when it comes to showing people upstanding, excellent character.

So I can be an example of what a young black man *really* is like. I give *all* women respect. I acknowledge them; I set an example. Because I want other guys to say, "Dr. Collins treats them well; he's never condescending." It *absolutely* affects it. Especially for those doctors who are junior to me. I want to send them a message—don't get caught up in that gentlemen's club mentality. It's okay to respond this way, and you will still get respect from other male doctors. (Emphasis in original.)

Weston's point here is that he has the position and the ability to have a positive impact on the how women are treated in medicine. Notably, he grounds this in his own recognition of the inequalities that shape U.S. society and the world more broadly—and in his own desire to present an image of upstanding black masculinity. Thus, treating women well—and setting an example for junior male doctors—allows him to highlight his character and to help improve how another minority group is treated in the medical field.

Interestingly, Weston's comment that it is possible to treat women professionally and capably while still retaining the respect of other men speaks to some of the recent literature on masculinity. Theorists in this area have argued that men's masculine behavior is largely for the benefit of other men and that women are merely props in men's efforts to prove themselves suitably masculine to other men.[26] Weston's acknowledgment of the "gaze" of other male doctors suggests that even as some black men actively work to improve women's standing in their field, these men are still concerned about behaving in a masculine way, which earns rewards and approval from other men.

Ronald, the civil engineering professor, also talks about making it a point to treat everyone equally:

In this country—well, this country for sure—women have traditionally had unnecessary and unfair bias placed upon them just because they are women. And then you add a minority card on top of it, and it's a little bit worse. And they tend to get underestimated more so. If you have a professional black man and a black woman, then they'll assume because he's a man that he is more qualified than she is, which may not be the case. Once you have been subjected to that sort of behavior, you tend to not exert any expectations on other people. You tend to learn to respect people just for who they are, and when you are respected for yourself, it doesn't matter what you are. Because I've been the subject of unfair treatment at times, and I tend not to do it to others because I know how it feels. I treat everybody pretty much the same.

Here, Ronald describes how the intersections of racism and sexism work to black women's disadvantage in fields like engineering. But he also shares, albeit very generally, that his experience with being prejudged and mistreated affects his interactions with women in engineering. Specifically, he tries to make it a point not to assume anything about women in the profession, an act that counters the low expectations they receive from others in the field.

These men describe various strategies that they use to try to help women colleagues and subordinates deal with the challenges and obstacles they encounter in male-dominated occupations. They recognize that gender creates difficulties for women colleagues, but at the same time, they understand gender also offers them—as men—opportunities to be taken more seriously and to fit in with the majority of other employees. Yet intersections of race and gender put black men in a position in which they also are intimately familiar with the indignity of being stereotyped, marginalized, and otherwise mistreated. Note the many respondents who describe identifying with women colleagues and recognizing the frustration that accompanies being misidentified or assumed to be less competent. These factors leave black men more attuned and responsive to the challenges that women face in these professions. Significantly, the men who fall into this category identify with women of various racial groups. While some acknowledge that black women face greater barriers to success because of their race and gender, these men felt that they could relate to both black and white women's experience in the minority.

This response, then, indicates one way in which partial tokenization affects the numerical minority's interaction with others. Black men in these professions are in the numerical minority and *do* experience some aspects of tokenization. However, being in the minority does not compel them to show loyalty to members of the dominant group.

Though they are aware that the male-dominated structure of their jobs offers them strategies to do this, rather than putting down their female coworkers to show solidarity with their white male colleagues, black men are more likely to use various techniques to advocate on the women's behalf. Instead of showing their loyalty to those in the dominant group, their own experiences with racial disadvantage create a sense of loyalty to another numerical minority.

This finding reveals marked differences from what Kris Paap uncovers in her study of the construction industry.[27] Like the men Paap observed, the men in my study work in a white male-dominated industry where they, and white women, are in the numerical minority.[28] However, whereas Paap finds that black men on the construction site often keep their distance from white women, the men I discuss here take a much more proactive role in not only interacting with their female counterparts but also attempting to challenge what they view as a difficult environment for women.[29]

The nature of the work in which these men are engaged may account for this difference. A key point Paap makes is that the disappearance of jobs in which working-class white men are well represented leads these men to see the construction industry as one of their few remaining "safe spaces."[30] Thus, many of the men she worked with went out of their way to construct the industry and job sites as havens where they could find freedom from women and people of color. She argues that this appeared to be a major factor that facilitated the harassment and negative treatment she and the few black men she worked with encountered.

In the professions in which my respondents work, these dynamics are possibly emerging but may not be as pronounced as Paap finds them to be in the construction industry.[31] The legal and medical fields are changing as the percentage of women graduating from law and medical schools increases. However, sex segregation still exists in these industries as women are overrepresented in "feminized" specializations within these fields. Thus, while women now make up the majority of those graduating from law school, they are still likely to pursue careers in family and child law rather than in litigation. Similarly, women are increasing their representation in medical school but are more likely to gravitate to family practice, obstetrics/gynecology, or pediatrics than the more male-dominated fields of emergency surgery or cardiology.

The men in my study are all concentrated in specializations that are still very white male–dominated (e.g., emergency medicine, investment banking, and mechanical engineering), with low numbers of women in their specific offices and subfields. Consequently, they are less likely to have encountered the sort of territoriality that Paap contends shapes the dynamics among white males, black males, and white women in the construction industry.[32]

It is also noteworthy that the methods and tactics these men use to make workplaces more equitable for their female colleagues appear to be free from the constraints of sexist ideology that can mar men's interactions with women. In their analysis of various forms of sexist behavior, Nijole Benokraitis and Joe Feagin describe condescending chivalry, radiant devaluation, and benevolent exploitation as pernicious forms of gender inequality because in these cases, even men's good-intentioned efforts to treat women well are still grounded in gendered ideas about women's fundamental inferiority to men.[33] In the cases described here, however, black professional men are not attempting to reinscribe women's subordinate status. Rather, they recognize that the hypermasculine culture of their workplaces contributes to a challenging environment for women colleagues. They are therefore motivated by their own experiences with racial inequality to address this.

Endorsing Dominant Group Ideology

Not all men, however, feel that women experience greater challenges than they do in these occupations. Some men in fact see certain women as having an edge. Most of these men concede that they work in very masculinized fields, but they also argue that within that space, there are opportunities for some women to create inroads to advancement.

Some of these men argue that intersections of race and gender allow white women to enjoy greater freedoms than black men. Nathan, the emergency room doctor, points to the experiences of a white female colleague to make this case:

> No one says that [they don't want to see a woman doctor], and sometimes women prefer a woman doctor for certain issues. You can imagine: we are in the South, and some women come in

and they have vaginal complaints or pelvic complaints, and, you know, they would prefer a woman doctor. And then if they were to get a doctor, I think the lowest—the last possible—person that they would want to see is a thirty-something-year-old black man. So I don't think she has the similar experience at all.

Though Nathan is undoubtedly correct that in some cases, female patients might prefer a woman doctor to treat certain ailments, it is unlikely that patients never express preferences for male physicians. Given the challenges faced by women in many historically male-dominated occupations, including but not limited to medicine, women doctors likely do encounter patients who openly doubt their capabilities and skills and prefer to be treated by men.[34] While I do not have data to evaluate whether the ranking system Nathan describes is accurate (i.e., that patients prefer white men, then white women, and black men least), he does seem to minimize the challenges that women encounter in the profession. As such, Nathan's assumption that women's experiences are completely dissimilar from his own may reflect a variation of Kanter's assertion that those in the minority turn against one another other.[35] While Nathan is not necessarily belittling or disparaging women, he does endorse some stereotypes about their experiences in the profession (i.e., the adage that they "have it easier") and fails to acknowledge the issues women face in male-dominated occupations.

Larry, the engineer, also describes working with a white female counterpart whose behavior leads him to believe that to a certain degree, women's experiences in these jobs are less difficult:

In a way, I think women may have it a little bit easier. Because I have to do [certain things] so I don't scare people. Because when people get scared, then they start talking: "See Larry; what's going on with him? Is he on drugs? Has he become a Muslim?" Women, they tend to be a little less threatening. A woman can get upset and go off. I can't even get upset and go off. I even had this older woman on one of my teams. She had twenty-five years service, so naturally she's more experienced in doing this kind of stuff than I am. And she's a white woman, and she's openly gay. So HR doesn't even have any set—they don't have a box to put her in. They won't touch her. So a lot of times she would just take over my meetings. And she's like, "You can kiss my ass, and you can tell your boss he can kiss my ass, because we're not going to do it." And she'd put her foot on the table. Kick her feet up on the table and sit back. "So what do you guys think about that?" And people would look at me like "Whoa!"

Interestingly, though Larry says elsewhere that he thinks women in general are not taken as seriously as men in engineering, he also notes that women have the advantage of accessing certain behaviors that are closed to him. In other words, he feels that women—particularly white women—are free to be brash and abrasive, whereas he is not permitted to "get upset and go off" for fear of scaring colleagues and playing into racialized, gendered fears about black men (this is discussed in more detail in Chapter 5).

Other men talk about how intersections of race and gender play out differently for black women. These men still contend that women, in some cases, had easier experiences in these jobs than did black men. Yet they also articulate ways that race and gender overlap to create opportunities for black women that reflect their social location both in the workplace and in the broader society.

Mitch, the emergency room doctor, is one respondent who speaks to this by comparing his experience to others:

I think that black women doctors actually have it a bit better. My wife is black, and she is a radiologist, she is a physician, and I think that she—I *know* that her experiences have been better. She does go through the same thing we go through, but I would not say she goes through it as often or as blatantly as we did. (Emphasis in original.)

Though Mitch cites his wife's experience to bolster his case that black women doctors face fewer difficulties than their black male counterparts, it is worth pointing out that his wife is a radiologist and would likely not encounter the same level and type of patient interaction that he does as an emergency room doctor. Many of the occupational challenges Mitch describes stem from patients having difficulty with being treated by a black doctor and his attempts to manage their discomfort to treat them effectively. Thus, he too may be indirectly endorsing the dominant viewpoint that those in the minority actually "have it easier." He is not overtly attempting to show loyalty to the dominant group, but he may nevertheless be tacitly employing their perspectives about those in the minority.

When asked to explain how he feels black women doctors cope with the issues they face, Mitch opines that they draw more from gender and racial solidarity than do white women physicians:

> Whereas the black women in medicine relate to each other and they stick together, and you got solidarity and camaraderie and that type of thing, what I've seen is that the other women who are in medicine—they want to be the same, like the guys. They want to be accepted and show that they can do as well as any guy can do, and they tend to compete with each other more than we [black men] do. Or more than black women do because black women stick together and help each other out. I know if you [other black women] mess up, you can be gone in a second. Or it will make it bad for me if you mess up, so we're going to help each other out. Whereas, . . . I would think they [white women] are more of the mind-set that they got to show the next person that they're as good [as] or better than anybody else, so they are very, very competitive. I know it's definitely harder for them. And that goes for black women too in the field. But like I said, black women will turn around to the other black women and say, "Have you dealt with so-and-so? He's kind of an ass," where the white woman doesn't have that other person to turn to.

Here, Mitch provides an analysis of the different ways intersections of race and gender affect black and white women in medicine. Though he is speculating, his argument points to how intersections of gender and race can work to help black women navigate a challenging work environment. While Mitch's observations suggest that black women can benefit from this gendered racial solidarity more so than their white peers, he also suggests that this can help make their experiences in the medical field less difficult.

Woody, the twenty-nine-year-old lawyer in a large firm, offers a similar contention about black women's experiences in the legal field:

> Black women's experience is different on a couple of levels. One, I think because there are more black females here than there are brothers. And two, I think females in general are more nurturing, and so by virtue of that, they look out for each other, and they actually care. They are going to make sure that sister girl is doing okay or whatever, whereas with guys, we're kind of like, "It's okay." Well, we're not okay. And that's just the kind of assumption guys make that I think makes it a harder experience for a young black male attorney. Because you really don't have more senior-type black male attorneys that's really taking the time to make sure you're okay.

Here, Woody offers an analysis similar to Mitch's. Both suggest that black women's "natural" nurturing tendencies enable them to help one another and provide much-needed social support. However, they also argue that this support enables black women to escape some of the obstacles that they, as black men, encounter in these jobs. Since black men assert that they do not have access to these critical social networks, these men are thus left to fend for themselves in work environments that they, like their black female colleagues, experience as hostile and challenging. This helps flesh out their claims that race and gender can create advantages for black women in these jobs but still downplays the difficulties that black women routinely cite in male-dominated positions.[36]

Other men argue that intersections of race and gender help black women gain access to certain jobs, although these men further argue that this did not necessarily translate into long-term occupational success. Rodney, a banking executive, offers this viewpoint when discussing the challenges he faces in getting assigned to important trips with clients:

> A couple of years ago, when I was still in the early stage of my job, . . . I spoke to two of my associates. . . . Both of them said in separate conversations that "if you were a black woman, you wouldn't even have this problem." They said it; I didn't. I think

it [being a black woman] would be easier in terms of getting into the door. That's—and I personally feel that's as far as it goes. I think that maybe as a black female—the idea is you get a two-for-one with a black female. Now once they get in the door, they're gonna have their own challenges being black and female. They're gonna still have that.

Rodney cites the common perception of black women as the "two-for-one" or "twofer," (two minorities in one) and suggests that this may help them in the early stages of accessing jobs, though not over the long term. Again, his claim belies the challenges black women encounter in professional positions, particularly in banking and finance.[37]

Finally, Terrance, a systems engineer, suggests that black women in his workplace have more opportunities for upward mobility:

I do sense that in our company, if you are a minority woman, you do, from a technology standpoint, you do get elevated. For instance, people who came when I first came in, in my training class, they elevated to second-line managers. . . . [I'm] not saying that they weren't capable, . . . but I do see that they have progressed fairly quickly in our organization, which is fine. . . . But I do feel that they get a little [kinder treatment]. You know, they're [a] minority and they're women, so we'll look at them, promote them, see if they want these opportunities. African American males—there's not too many role models there, and if they are, they're not vocal. You kind of have to seek them out, because I think they're pretty much grinding like us, trying to stay afloat. And so a few I've reached out to—they've been pretty open to talking and helping out, but it's not like, you know, they're going to be on front street, saying, "Here I am; come everybody and talk to me." You have to kind of make an effort to reach out to them.

Terrance thus goes further than Rodney in arguing that black women's advantages extend past the initial hiring stages. In his observations, the few black women in his company generate extra attention, whereas black men lack the mentorship that would put them in line for similar opportunities. Again, though I do not have data on Terrance's company, the idea that black women are rapidly promoted does not correspond with the research documenting the extensive challenges these women face in professional positions.

The examples black men cite here contradict the accounts of respondents who contend that women face greater challenges in predominantly male occupations. Respondents like Rodney and Terrance suggest instead that intersections of race and gender work to make women's occupational experiences easier in the male-dominated workplace. Significantly, the idea that those in the minority "have it easier" and have not had to display the same level of fortitude or amount of work, commitment, and effort as others reflects typical tropes that those in the dominant group use to suggest minorities are less deserving of their positions. While these men do not make these statements in an effort to pass loyalty tests and gain favor with those in the dominant group, they are nonetheless endorsing some aspects of dominant-group ideology.

Given this, I argue that the experience of tokenization does not fully describe how these men respond and relate to women in their professions. The men who are skeptical of the challenges women face do not openly rail against them or behave dismissively toward them as a way of proving their loyalty. Inasmuch as they experience partial tokenization, however, these men are more likely to see women colleagues as people who have opportunities that they do not because of the various manifestations of the intersections of race and gender. Moreover, these black men are relatively comfortable supporting dominant group ideologies about those in the numerical minority receiving unfair advantages.

Self-Quarantine

Finally, Kanter argues that the "quarantine" is a factor in how dominant groups treat tokens.[38] As discussed previously, she argues that tokens are quarantined when they are isolated from members of the dominant group. This is part of the social dynamic that pushes tokens to try to demonstrate their loyalty to the dominant group. Were black men to experience the quarantine process, they might describe incidents in which they, along with white women, were excluded from important meetings and interactions. Or they might contend that by virtue of racial solidarity, white women were included as part of the dominant group and joined with white men in quarantining the black men from key social functions. Yet a third possibility is black men capitalizing on their gender ties to white male dominants and actively (or subtly) attempting to informally isolate women from group interactions. Kanter focuses primarily on how the quarantine process pushes dominant groups to exclude tokens, but when there are several groups that constitute a numerical minority, it stands to reason that there are different possibilities for how quarantining might play out.[39]

Here, I suggest that black men's experiences interacting with other tokens reveal a process that could more accurately described as a "self-quarantine." More specifically, when associating with women in the workplace, some black men respondents argue for the need to keep their distance. This differs from Kanter's conceptualization because these men are not describing a process in which members of the dominant group push them—the black men—into a separate space.[40] Rather, black men's experience with partial tokenization means that they choose to distance themselves from some women colleagues. Additionally, they are driven to engage in the self-quarantine because of the effects of the intersections of race and gender on them as black men interacting with white women.

Michael, the engineering professor, talks about engaging in the process of self-quarantining when it comes to interacting with female coworkers:

> I will say that I watch what I do with female counterparts probably far more than my white colleagues. I think, in general, there is—you know, people are always watching black colleagues, so I'm very careful with how I interact with female students or female colleagues so that things cannot be interpreted the wrong way. Because if they are, it will be a very negative interpretation. Like my male colleagues, we'll run down to the bank. No big deal. Get in the car and drive to the bank. I would never do that with a female colleague. As a matter of fact, I had [a female colleague] my first year. She said, "I can't even joke with you." She was a little my senior—very nice, very helpful. [She'd say things like] "Michael, want to go out to dinner? I'm taking my son,"

blah, blah, blah. We were going to go out to dinner, and I was like, "Yeah—let me call my wife." So while if it had been a male colleague, it would have been fine [if I hadn't brought my wife], but with a female colleague, I could have never gotten away with it. Especially since she was a white female colleague. I could have had a big mess with that. So I keep an eye on that.

While other men in male or female-dominated jobs may be cautious about interactions with women for fear of lawsuits, misunderstandings, or charges of sexual harassment, it is important to underscore that for Michael, much of his vigilance is shaped by the intersections of race and gender. As a black male, he is well aware of the long history and graphic imagery of relationships between black men and white women, which has usually been used in the cultural imagination to suggest rape, to provide legitimization for violence toward black men, and to cover up the much more frequent dynamic of white male sexual aggression toward black women.[41] Thus, while Michael's white male colleagues might also be reluctant to dine alone with a female colleague, it is unlikely that their hesitation stems from racialized, gendered representations of themselves as sexual predators or from the challenges that accompany being in the racial minority. These particular factors, and how they reflect specific aspects of race and gender, make Michael very careful about engaging in any behaviors that could evoke this ugly stereotype.

Michael argues that this wariness extends to female students as well as colleagues. This carries a bit of a different dynamic, given that in graduate programs, students often depend on strong relationships with professors to gain critical publishing experience, research and teaching assistantships, and other key positions that help advance careers. He acknowledges that this cautiousness can work to female students' disadvantage, as they are not privy to mentoring, close attention, and the kind of personal relationships that he offers male students. Thus, this type of behavior is a bit more similar to Kanter's original conceptualization, wherein those who are left out can miss critical information that allows for job stability or even upward mobility.[42] However, Michael insists that this is necessary given the dynamics of being a black male interacting with white women in a predominantly white male environment:

I never close a door with female students. For some reason, they're all coming in to talk to me, and I'm not quite sure why. You know, I think I'm a good-looking guy [*laughing*], but it will always be perceived in the wrong way if I'm closing this door behind a female student or anything like that. And I may be actually doing some—not damage but not being fair to my female students, because they don't get the same level of personal contact that my male students do, or I'm a little more reserved with them. Like my male students, I'll be much more frank with them, whereas female students might need that, and sometimes I hesitate to give that. Or I would think nothing of taking a male graduate student—"Hey, you going to the airport for the conference? Yeah, you can ride with me," or something. But I would think twice about taking a female student, and it would make life harder on her. She wouldn't get the same benefit, but I wouldn't give her that offer just because of how it would be perceived.

Again, Michael identifies how intersections of gender and race create a relatively unique experience for black men in these occupations. Men of other racial groups may be skittish about their interactions, but Michael's is particularly shaped by the image of black men as sexual predators. Thus, while black men's partial tokenization enables them to see and empathize with the gender-related challenges women face in male-dominated jobs, this certainly has its limits. Race and gender put them in a position in which they understand and relate to the obstacles women face and are able to make some efforts to address them. However, the other side of these intersections is that they reinforce distance between black men and white women in these jobs.

Nathan, the emergency room doctor, offers a similar account. He works at a hospital and describes employing this level of caution when interacting with the mostly white female nursing staff there:

I joke around at work, and we all have a good camaraderie, and there's a lot of people who are all in the similar age group, and we all joke with each other. But as far as joking with some of the nurses and some of the staff, I joke a little bit, but some people joke to a different level. Me, personally—I just feel like if someone were ever to get offended, it looks worse if it's coming from [me] versus coming from a person [who's white]. [It's this] flirtatious joking type thing. You know, I keep it strictly professional. For me, I just feel that that's probably not appropriate. I mean, it is appropriate in our workplace. I'm not chastising anybody who does that, but you just have to be careful of who you joke with, how you joke, and how that joke is perceived. Because if someone else does it, it's going to be swept under the rug. When you do it, someone's going to [have a different reaction]. . . . A perfect example is this: If someone else said a joke that was inappropriate or did something that was inappropriate, they would say, "Hey, dude, that wasn't funny; it's kind of inappropriate." And then he would say, "All right, I'm sorry," and that would be the end of it. If [I] did it, it would be, "Hey, that was inappropriate!" They would tell the supervisor, who would tell you to write a formal complaint, write it on paper, submit it, two people sign it, your witnesses sign it, and then turn it in. So that's where it's different.

Nathan indicates that race and gender put him in a position such that sexualized banter with white women nurses is off-limits. This is not an established rule of the hospital but one that he imposes on himself given the underlying context of historical and cultural interactions between black men and white women—and his sense that any infractions (real or perceived) would lead to greater disciplinary action for him. He also goes further to describe how he exempts himself from situations that have the potential for this sort of flirtatious undertone:

When things get to an uncomfortable level, I just tend to either walk away or not answer. You just try not to get yourself involved. [Because when someone complains] and the supervisor or whoever asks, "Who was there?" [The response] is "three nurses and the black guy." You always stand out a little bit, so you always get noticed. Whether you say something or you don't say something, they always remember that you're in the vicinity and you're there. So it's just better to leave.

Here, Nathan gives a clear example of the concept of self-quarantining. When sexualized jokes or comments arise, he simply chooses to extricate himself from the situation. Unlike the process Kanter describes in which those in the numerical minority are isolated and excluded by members of the dominant group, Nathan is voluntarily choosing to walk away from others who are also in the minority.[43] Yet his reasons for doing so are largely shaped by these intersections of race and gender and how they facilitate images of highly sexualized black men.

Richard, another doctor, gives an account that echoes Nathan's concerns about interacting with nurses:

> There's a lot of innuendo that goes on between nurses and doctors in the ER. Sexual innuendo. I joke around and have fun, but I have a line that I don't cross with my jokes or my interactions or my comments. I have a line I just don't cross so there is no question as to what the hell is going on. I'm just careful. But you see [other doctors and nurses doing] crazy things. I'm just careful about doing those because I'll be damned if it ruins my career.

As Richard describes them, interactions with mostly white female nurses warrant extreme caution. They have the potential for misunderstanding, miscommunication, and, ultimately, serious problems. While he describes seeing other doctors and nurses interacting in a much more intimate manner (at another point in our interview, he discusses a doctor and nurse who had been having an affair, subsequently had a bad breakup, and proceeded to yell at each other in the emergency room), like Nathan, he was clear that this was not an option for him. Though he did not describe taking the steps Nathan or Michael did of actively removing himself from interactions with white women, his words make clear that he was very structured in his relationships with these colleagues.

Summary

The theory of tokenism posits that those in the numerical minority are pushed to turn against one another, but it does not say much about how different minority groups interact with one another. Analyzing black professional men's relationships with women reveals a complicated picture of how these men interact with others in the minority. Many respondents talk about the sense of solidarity they feel with women workers, rather than simply showing loyalty to the dominant group by emphasizing gender solidarity. These respondents are able to identify and relate to the processes that keep women of all races from fully integrating into the dominant group. In some cases, they even go further to try to create opportunities and avenues to help women succeed against institutional odds.

This aspect of men's interactions with women reveals both how race and gender intersect to shape occupational experiences and how the gendering of the occupation matters. As black men, these respondents are both insiders and outsiders in the workplace. Their gender—and the fact that they work in male-dominated jobs—enables them to enjoy some privileges. They observe that because they are in male-dominated industries, their masculinity makes them part of the dominant group. Yet race and gender intersect so that they are constantly aware of how they differ from the white males who constitute the bulk of their co-workers and supervisors. Additionally, these intersecting factors cause some black men to develop a sense of affinity and sympathy for the challenges their women colleagues face, and they use the benefits of being men in "masculine" jobs to advocate for women, whom they see as being denigrated by the gendered occupational culture.

The ways that black men engage and interact with women colleagues suggests that some of the challenges they face as black professionals may perhaps motivate them to try to create more equitable work environments. The existing literature in this area documents the issues of discrimination, marginalization, and isolation that many black professional workers encounter.[44] Yet there is not much discussion of how these experiences motivate black professionals to effect structural change that can make their workplaces more equitable. This research shows that black professional men in masculinized jobs *do* encounter some challenges (though these are mediated by the intersections of race and gender). Significantly, however, the obstacles that they face compel them to use their relative power as men within the organization to establish a fairer, more level playing field for women of all racial groups, whom they see as disadvantaged in ways that resemble the challenges they themselves face.

But not all men follow this path. Some respondents' experiences are more similar to the phenomenon Kanter describes when those in the numerical minority turn against others.[45] These respondents do not go so far as to describe women colleagues as "enemies" or impediments to their progress and upward mobility, but they do see women as people who benefit from the institutional and occupational norms in the workplace, and they frequently understate the challenges that researchers show are likely to confront women who work in male-dominated environments.[46] Here, some of the tensions and dissension that Kanter describes among tokens are present, although muted.[47]

Once again, in this context, intersections of race and gender influence the experience of being in the numerical minority. Black male workers identify race and gender as factors that work to the benefit of women employees at their expense. Remember that both Rodney and Terrance argue that intersections of race and gender work to the advantage of women of color, putting them in a more visible position for hiring and possibly promotion as well. Men who adopt this viewpoint rarely articulate a perception that intersections of race and gender work to their benefit in the same way. In contrast, their take is that as black men, they are hindered while women see gains as a consequence of these intersecting factors. The fact that they are employed in male-dominated jobs comes into play here as well because these men assert that the gender dynamics of the workplace heighten women's visibility and lead to opportunities from which they are excluded.

Finally, the process of quarantining that Kanter describes is manifested in a more complicated fashion when we examine the experiences of black male professionals.[48] Rather than being isolated by those in the dominant group, some black men engage in what I describe as a self-quarantine. They choose voluntarily to distance themselves from women, particularly white women, in a conscious attempt to structure and control both their interactions with these women and the ways that they are perceived by others.

The self-quarantine reveals another way that the dynamics of race and gender work to shape the experience of being in the numerical minority. As black men, the respondents are well aware of the stereotypes and imagery that cast them as threats to white women's purity and respectability. Consequently, they are very careful to avoid behavior—or even the appearance of behavior—that might play into or evoke these cultural references. As Michael notes, this type and level of caution may work to the continued disadvantage of women in these fields, but the respondents who engaged in the self-quarantine viewed it as a necessary behavior.

The complicated relationships black men have with women in these professions indicate that race and gender intersect to create more nuance in the experience of tokenization than is offered through existing research. Specifically, these overlapping factors coupled with work in a male-dominated job lead black men to experience partial tokenization that shapes how they interact with women at work. More so than the concept of tokenization, then, the idea of partial tokenization helps to explain the complicated interactions black men can have with women in male-dominated, professional jobs. As partial tokens, these men may experience a level of solidarity or empathy with women workers rather than feeling the need to distance themselves to show loyalty to the dominant group. Conversely, they may feel a sense of disunity that manifests itself in the belief that women have greater advantages, while overlooking the challenges and problems women face in a white male–dominated environment. Finally, partial tokenization contributes to self-quarantining, in which black male workers do not experience rejection (isolation) from the dominant group but feel compelled to isolate themselves from others in the numerical minority (white women, specifically) to avoid potential problems and misunderstandings.

4 | Other Men in the Workplace

In Chapter 3, I focus on the various aspects of the relationships black professional men have with women in the workplace. Women make up a very small percentage of the workforce in these work environments, and they are infrequently in positions of power and influence in the male-dominated professions. This being the case, professional black men are much more likely to interact with other men when they are at work. They relate to and develop ties with male colleagues differently from how they forge connections with women coworkers. However, connections to other men at work are still a critical part of the dynamic of these men's professional lives. I now turn to an examination of the ways that being in the numerical minority influences black men's interactions with both white and other black men.

New Methods of Contrasts

In Chapter 3, I recount Rosabeth Moss Kanter's discussion of how dominant groups establish contrasts between themselves and tokens as a means of reinforcing tokens' outsider status.[1] When interacting with women, black men use variations of the quarantine and are less concerned about displaying loyalty to the dominant group. These processes are shaped by intersections of race and gender as well as by the context of working in "masculine" jobs. When it comes to interacting with other men at work, however, contrasting still occurs but in different ways.

In addition to the quarantine and loyalty tests, Kanter contends that members of the dominant group may establish contrasts between themselves and tokens by exaggerating their differences.[2] She describes male executives engaged in crass sexual banter and joking as a means of emphasizing the differences between themselves and the women present:

> Around token women, then, men sometimes exaggerated displays of aggression and potency: instances of sexual innuendos, aggressive sexual teasing, and prowess-oriented "war stories." When a woman or two were present, the men's behavior involved "showing off," telling stories in which "masculine prowess" accounted for personal, sexual, or business success. They highlighted what they could do, as men, in contrast to the women.[3]

This serves to highlight the cultural differences between men and women and reinscribe the women as outsiders.

A specific tactic dominant group members may use to establish contrasts between themselves and tokens involves interrupting group events, practices, or settings to highlight the presence of those in the numerical minority. As with stressing cultural differences, interruptions serve to remind tokens that they do not completely fit into the dominant group. Tokens are expected to sanction this "normal," presumably ordinary behavior that the dominants are engaging in, which tokens might consider offensive or problematic. Of this process, Kanter writes:

> Dominants prefaced acts with apologies or questions about appropriateness directed at the token; they then invariably went ahead with the act, having placed the token in the position of interrupter or interloper, of someone who took up the group's time. . . . At the same time, tokens have also been given the implicit message that majority members do *not* expect those forms of expression to be "natural" to the tokens' home culture; otherwise, majority members would not need to raise the question.[4]

The process lets those in the majority reinforce their dominant position, while simultaneously putting those in the minority in the awkward position of sanctioning behaviors that marginalize them.

As discussed previously, Kanter focuses exclusively on women who are tokens in male-dominated environments.[5] However, it is not difficult to theorize about how these processes might manifest themselves for black men who are in the numerical minority in predominantly white male workplaces. Black men could still presumably face encounters with white male workers who attempt to exaggerate differences by drawing unnecessary attention to black employees' race. This can occur through white workers stating that black workers are not really expected to succeed or flourish in the workplace or needlessly identifying their racial characteristics rather than their professional accomplishments. Indeed, the literature on black professionals is rife with examples of this sort. In their study of the black middle class, Joe Feagin and Melvin Sikes quote a drug abuse counselor who describes ways white coworkers highlight his racial status as a marker of difference:

> I was working in a predominantly white hospital. And I feel as though the way I was discriminated against was I always got considered or got identified as "that black counselor up on that unit." . . . That always qualified my experience, it always qualified my expertise, or either it discredited it, I should say. "Well, that's John, that black guy upstairs on that unit." So I had to always fight through that, and as a result, I ended up always having to deal with people being able to accept my credibility.[6]

As this counselor's example shows, black professionals who are in the minority are subject to dealing with members of the dominant group who actively exaggerate differences as a means of underscoring the contrasts between those in the majority and those in the minority.

While we might expect to see cases like this, surprisingly few surface. Black men interviewed for this project rarely cite incidents in which white male colleagues attempted to establish contrasts with them through the processes Kanter describes.[7] In her study of black men and white women in the leveraged buyout industry, Catherine Turco finds

similar results and explains them by arguing that the cultural foundations of this industry are more gendered than they are racialized.[8] While
this may be true to some extent, it does not explain why black male
workers in certain white male–dominated occupations do not feel fully
integrated into their predominantly white male workplaces. Nor does it
explain the how they *do* perceive contrasts between themselves and their
white male coworkers. I argue here that the processes that serve to establish contrasts between black male workers and their white counterparts
are more structural than interactional. In particular, black men contend
that the structural processes of developing social networks to aid their
advancement and upward mobility play a significant part in creating
contrasts between black men and their white male counterparts.

Social Networks and Contrasts

Nearly all respondents acknowledge that social networks play a critical role in helping them establish connections and create forward movement in their chosen professions. These networks help lawyers establish
a strong clientele, bankers cultivate relationships with customers, doctors land desirable positions, and engineers work on key projects that
help advance their careers. Yet respondents talk a great deal about the
differences they observe in their own integration into important social
networks versus the integration of their white male colleagues.

For lawyers, this is a particularly acute issue. Succeeding as a partner
in a firm is often contingent on building a "book of business," through
which attorneys cultivate and maintain relationships with clients who
bring revenue into the firm. However, this aspect of their work is often
heavily driven by the social networks in which they are included. Regardless of educational, class, or social background, most black men do
not have ties to established white business owners through whom they
might potentially build this book of business. Attorney Warren talks
about facing this predicament:

> My challenge is not within the firm. The challenge I see as a black
> man is in the legal community in terms of clients. Most business
> relationships are based on the [personal] relationship. And a lot
> of them are based clearly on friendship or social relationships—

our quote, unquote "rainmakers." It's not because they're the best lawyers; they just have friends—they just happen to have their best friends as the GC [General Counsel] of this company, or their best friend is the CEO of this company. So that opens up business for them, and they are seen as more valuable in terms of bringing dollars in the door. And that's where you see the challenge because my social network prior to arriving [here] doesn't include any people that fit that description. I didn't grow up with anybody who's the CEO somewhere. And my colleagues in college—and I tended to not branch out as much as I should have, and so it's mostly a circle, up until I get to my professional career, of all black people, who are, again, less likely to be in the decision-making role. They're not plugged in to those companies. So I don't have the connection that I see some of my peers having and able to have, [to] hit the ground running. I'm grinding and trying to build those relationships and doing a whole lot of networking and stuff to try and get there.

As Warren articulates, the barriers that are erected between him and his white male colleagues are not as straightforward or intentional as those Kanter describes.[9] Rather, these distances exist because of a lack of social ties that would enable Warren to advance professionally at the same pace as his white male peers. Contrasts are not established through overt, intentional processes but through his realization that his white colleagues have critical connections to which he does not share access.

Randy, another attorney, makes a remark very similar to Warren's observation. He too argues that his limited access to certain social networks enhances the contrasts between him and his colleagues:

[As a black man], if you've developed a book of business, it's yours. You've developed it. You've nourished it. You've gone out and beat the bushes and brought it back. Didn't nobody give it to you. Didn't nobody assist you in getting it. That's your baby. And I certainly understand and respect the black men that I've worked with over the years, and they work hard. Whatever client they had, didn't nobody give it to them. They had to go out and hustle for it, compete for it—and they landed it. White cats—there's this fellowship; there's this cronyism; there's this understanding that what's mine is mine and yours is yours. With white guys, it's "I'm going to go out here and get this piece of business; by the way, when I get it, I'm going to give you [other white guys] a little piece of it. And when I'm gone, I'm going to pass it on to you, and then you can pass it on to some folks, and we're going to work this thing and do better, collectively do it." [With black men], brother, you going to do it all yourself. You're going to do it by yourself. You're out there by yourself. And you don't have the same entry to get the best in the world.

Echoing Warren, Randy draws a line between how his networks allow him to build business versus how his white colleagues' networks allow them to grow business. Like many of the other men interviewed for this study, Randy does not describe a work environment in which white men go out of their way to establish contrasts between themselves and their black male colleagues. However, this is not to say that contrasts are not felt. Men like Randy note contrasts between themselves and white male coworkers based on the differences in the two groups' social networks.

My research suggests that awareness of the differences in mentorship, social ties, and networks can heighten the contrasts between black men and their white male peers. Significantly, the men who cite this type of contrasting do not argue that differences are highlighted through active effort from white men in the workplace. Instead, the existence of these different networks—and the consequences that arise from them—is what creates a sense of contrast between black men in the minority and the dominant group.

Bonding with White Men

In keeping with black men's argument that white men do not always overtly attempt to highlight the contrasts between them, many respondents talk about their perception that the lines of work in which they are employed actually allow them to develop ties and augment their similarities to white male colleagues relatively easily. In particular, many men argue that the male-dominated nature of their jobs allows for increased bonding based on gendered interests. This allows them to enhance their similarities to white men and helps explain why these men do not cite frequent instances of the contrasting Kanter describes.[10]

Kojo, the sixty-two-year-old lawyer for a major corporation, states point blank that being male makes it easier to bond with other male coworkers in some capacities: "Just based on where we are in the United States of America, and, to a degree, being a male—that's probably, in some instances, even to an advantage. Because some guys feel more comfortable dealing with males."

Kojo is straightforward in his assessment that men's comfort with other men can help black men professionally. Again, like other men quoted in this study, he does not offer examples of how white male colleagues seek to establish contrasts. Rather, Kojo indicates that the gendered composition of black men's jobs enables them to establish some inroads with white men.

Michael, the engineering professor at a highly ranked research university, compares his experiences to those of women to show how doing "men's work" has helped him bond with white men:

> If you're male and African American, you don't have the double bias [that women face]. You're a minority, but you can befriend the other male colleagues. And maybe they won't like you, but there are enough senior male colleagues that one of them will like you, and you can get the information you need. So it's much different for a female [of any race] to come into this department than an African American male, because I'm a male, and a lot of the restrictions that male colleagues will put on their interactions with females in the department don't exist [for me]. They may have their [racial] biases, but they can openly communicate with me. We can travel together. We can share accommodations. We can go to lunch together, and nothing will ever be construed of it.

Michael's juxtaposition of his experience with that of his women colleagues highlights the various ways black men can bond with white men in these jobs. Since engineering is overwhelmingly comprised of male workers, as Michael points out, the luck of the numbers means that at some point, he will encounter another male colleague with whom he gets along and can develop a working relationship. Additionally, opportunities to travel and enjoy other social activities together facilitate bonding with white male colleagues. These connections can explain why black men do not encounter the heightened contrasts Kanter describes.[11] Because they have the chance to form relationships with white men through various professional and social activities, black men may not often find that white male colleagues actively enhance the contrasts between them.

Ronald, the civil engineering professor, makes this point as well. In discussing friends he has made through work, he too cites his work in a job primarily dominated by men as a factor in his ability to form ties with white male coworkers:

> One of [my friendships was established] through working out. I work out with an associate dean. We work out every morning, and we talk every morning and have coffee together in the morning. And that's one of the differences between—I think the advantages that men have, like just working out.

Here, Ronald touches on the subtle ways in which black men form relationships with white men that are unavailable to women, no matter their race. Though women can and do work out and exercise, black men have special access to white male peers and superiors in the locker room, sauna, and other gendered spaces that are closed to women workers. As Ronald shows, this closed space enabled him to develop a friendship with a white male in a more powerful, higher-status position.

The experiences these men describe offer an interesting parallel to other studies that discuss the various processes of tokenism. In particular, Williams's study of mostly white male tokens in female-dominated jobs reveals a somewhat similar paradigm of male camaraderie.[12] Studying men working as nurses, social workers, librarians, and teachers, Williams observes that the ability to establish relationships and close ties with mostly male supervisors offers the male tokens opportunities that are often unavailable to their female counterparts, even though women are in the numerical majority in these jobs.[13] Significantly, this experience of bonding with white male supervisors is *not* replicated in a subsequent study of black men working in nursing, a female-dominated profession.[14] Yet for black men who work in male-dominated professions, like engineering, law, and the like, it appears that they may have access to these gendered relationships, which facilitate opportunities and, potentially, advancement. Although black men, like white women, are in the numerical minority, black men's work in a gendered—specifically, male—occupation allows them to bond with white men rather than face the contrasting that Kanter attributes to tokens.[15]

Ties to Higher-Status White Men

While black men in gendered occupations experience relatively easy bonding with white male colleagues, it is worth exploring how they develop ties to white men who are in positions of power. According to Kanter's arguments, similar processes of contrasting should be present here as well.[16] Other studies indicate that racial bias limits black men's opportunities to develop relationships with white male supervisors and bosses. For instance, in her analysis of the challenges facing black male and white female attorneys, Jennifer Pierce reveals that black men can face serious obstacles when they seek mentorship and support from senior white male colleagues.[17] In Pierce's account, Randall Kingsley, a black male lawyer, describes white male senior attorneys who avoid lunch dates with him, decline his requests for mentorship, and fail to provide the necessary support for success in the field. Further, these white attorneys who exclude him do so based on assertions that Kingsley is "too flashy," "demanding," and couldn't "fit in."[18] Without this critical support from senior associates, Kingsley faced enormous challenges in the firm and ultimately chose to leave to pursue opportunities elsewhere.

Black professional men in my study often tell a different story. As I describe, many of them argue that they benefit from working in gendered occupations because they are able to develop connections to other men. Furthermore, many black men take advantage of these gender dynamics to form ties to white male colleagues and supervisors. In fact, they describe this as absolutely necessary for occupational success and advancement. Inasmuch as black male workers are aware of how white men's networks form more of a significant contrast than everyday workplace interactions, they are also attuned to the fact that having solid relationships with higher-status white men is often critical to their professional careers. Thus, many respondents talk freely about the importance of developing ties to white men in higher-status positions than the ones they hold, and they are forthcoming about how these connections have helped them at work.

Jason, a high-ranking attorney at a major corporation, talks openly about the fact that success in his profession depends on the endorsement of an even higher-ranking, usually white male worker:

> There's this whole notion in corporate America and perhaps in academia and perhaps in other places—this idea that you have to be made by somebody. The idea that you had to be made by somebody and that we have to have—call them mentors, call them rabbis, call them whatever you call them—but this reality that our success is formed not just by hard work and not just by a rosy disposition and not just by a diligent navigator and not just by a level of, you know, social and emotional intelligence but that somebody on high has basically got us under his wing—and the world knows that.

Here, Jason emphasizes that hard work and talent are simply not sufficient for black men. The critical factor—and one that he acknowledges has been a factor in his own career—is the support from influential white men.

Jared, the forty-seven-year-old engineering professor, also shares how ties to a white male mentor have helped his career:

> For me and probably a lot of African Americans, we can't lean on a family member who has had a similar [professional] experience and say, "You know, Dad was teaching at whatever." In my family, on either side of my family, as far as we know, I'm the only doctorate. So therefore, I'm the only professor. So there's certain sort of rules of thumb, learning the ropes; there's certain tricks of the trade that I have to get from the job or colleagues here. There's no family I can go to to say, "Oh yeah, tell me about it." [And] depending on how, as a grad student, your adviser is in sharing things, you still may not get information. 'Cause sometimes they share a lot and you get to learn a lot, and sometimes they don't and there's a lot of things that you don't

know. You may be very good at conducting research in the lab, taking data, analyzing it, and doing calculations, but depending on your experience as a graduate student, you may not get a good feel for what the life of a professor is and how to optimize that and what things to think about and do. So in that sense, it was important to have somebody who was more experienced, whom I could trust—someone that I could go to and say, "Hey, you know, what about this? What about that?" So, yes, it's been helpful in terms of just helping my performance and what I'm doing and that sort of thing.

Jared's statements here highlight how race and class can intersect to create an occupational experience for black professional men wherein good mentorship is absolutely necessary. Black Americans have historically been underrepresented in many professional positions. Indeed, as of 2001, black men constituted only 3 percent of the nation's professors, so Jared's experience being the only one on either side of his family is hardly unique.[19] Given this, being able to talk openly with and rely on a senior faculty member who knew the ins and outs of the professoriate was integral to his professional advancement.

Lionel, the doctor whose grandmother was a nurse, also talks about the critical role his white male mentor played in his career trajectory:

[My mentor is] the person who hired me, basically. He's no longer here, actually, so he's still one of my mentors. He actually helped recruit me here and said, "I want you to help grow and develop this department"—those kinds of things. So I would say almost all that's professional mentorship in terms of how to grow my academic career and portfolio and something to work on. We still keep in contact in terms of growth, development. He looks out for me and does the things that you want a mentor to do—sort of look for opportunity, feedback, say, "I'd do this differently" and this kind of thing, and be honest and open about it. He's probably the one that I would say truly operates in that mentor role. I have people that I have close relationships with and will do many of those kind of things, but he's probably the one that does that the most.

Like Jason and Jared, Lionel speaks warmly of this mentor and acknowledges the important role this person has played in his upward mobility.

The opportunities for bonding and mentoring relationships that these respondents describe offer an interesting dissimilarity to Kanter's description of how those in the numerical minority face challenges from the dominant group.[20] According to her theorization, these men should face regular instances of "contrasting" from white male colleagues. However, rather than interrupt interactions to emphasize black men's racial status or exaggerate presumed differences between them, contrasts are primarily felt indirectly. Black men are aware of the contrasts between themselves and their white colleagues as they grow to understand the more extensive social networks their white peers can access. More important, they note that working in male-dominated jobs offers them opportunities to develop critical ties to higher-status white men that are invaluable in getting ahead at work. Thus, the gendered character of their jobs proves invaluable in formulating important interracial connections.

In this manner, the fact that these men are employed in gendered occupations works to their advantage and shapes how they experience partial tokenization. They feel the contrasts between themselves and those in the dominant group, but these contrasts are established through structural rather than interactional processes. Additionally, working in gendered, male occupations enables them to form ties that mitigate the differences between themselves and white male colleagues and helps facilitate job success.

Interacting with Other Black Men

For black men in these jobs, most of the male colleagues they have are white men (though some engineers work with several Asian American male coworkers). However, most respondents either know—or more rarely, work with—one or two other black men in their professions. This provides an important occupational dynamic to consider. Kanter theorizes that the social pressures members of the minority face lead them to turn against those in their group.[21] In particular, as tokens encounter the dominant group's efforts to highlight the contrasts between them, tokens are pushed to renounce their connections to one another and work to curry favor with members of the dominant group. In the previous chapter, I demonstrate that this paradigm does not always hold true between minority groups, as many black men establish ties with women colleagues rather than turn against them. In this section, I address whether this pattern reveals itself among black men. As members of the numerical minority, do black men, as Kanter predicts, "try to become insiders, proving their loyalty by defining themselves as exceptions and turning against their own social category"?[22]

The short answer to this question appears to be that they do not. Rather than attempting to ingratiate themselves with the majority of their white male coworkers and supervisors by turning against or attempting to differentiate themselves from other black male workers, respondents cite a sense of solidarity with the other black males. In some ways, this is similar to the sense of connection that black men describe with women colleagues, in that they identify with those who are not in the dominant group and who have to deal with the consequences of that social subordination. However, black men's solidarity with other black men is often more fundamental and deeply rooted than the ties they feel to women colleagues. While black men feel they can relate to the challenges women face, with other black men, they feel a sense that these are people who truly understand and relate to the unique experiences they encounter as black men in predominantly white professional settings.

Mitch, the emergency room doctor, talks about the important role his ties to other black male coworkers plays in his daily work life:

> In my emergency department, in my group, there's sixteen physicians and there's three of us—three black men all under the age of forty. And we all kind of go through the same [thing]: we share our stories. It does increase a sense of camaraderie with them. Yeah, if there's a day where there's three of us on—just the three of us—we can sit around and talk about, obviously, things that you don't talk about around your white colleagues. So yeah, in our office, we've got our little iPod stereo that sits in there, and we don't bring our music in unless it's the three of us. I'm not going to sit in the office and play Bob Marley or play whatever with the rest of them [white colleagues] just because it wouldn't be acceptable. It would probably be considered unprofessional.

But, you know, amongst us, it's okay because we all know that you don't have to fit a social norm or conformity to be good at what you do, to be professional. We talk a lot; we go out a lot. We share things with each other that we don't share with other people we work with. [For instance,] some of our business ventures that we don't talk about with other people [and] trying to find ways to make it to where everybody wants to be, and it's something that you can't talk about with other people.

Mitch works in a rather unusual setting, in which nearly 20 percent of the doctors in his department are black men. Yet he clearly illustrates that this leads him and his fellow coworkers to draw together rather than working to show their differences. In particular, these men provide one another with a much-needed release valve at work: they can be themselves, share honest feelings and emotions, and talk candidly about the challenges their jobs provide. Given that elsewhere in his interview, Mitch shared he is routinely subjected to racial slurs from patients who do not want to be treated by a black doctor, it is critical that he is able to feel a sense of camaraderie and connection to his fellow black colleagues who have similar experiences and can provide sounding boards for one another.

Nathan, one of the other emergency room doctors, echoes Mitch's sentiments about the importance of interacting with other black men who can relate to their experiences:

It's just nice to know that someone else has a shared experience. I felt when you're in a workplace and it's just Caucasians or, you know, non–African Americans, they don't tend to believe, or some of the things that happen they don't believe happened, but you know that it happens all the time. For example, I had a patient complaint, and the complaint was—one of the supervisors came and said, "I want to tell you something. We had a patient complaint—some lady that you saw February of '08. She came in and she complained; she made a complaint." And I was like, "Why a year later?" And she said, "That's the strangest thing. She said that she requested a white doctor, and there was a black doctor." And [the supervisor] was like, "Can you believe that?" And she was astonished! And I was like, "Yeah, I believe that. It happens all the time." Now, they [other black male doctors] don't have that sense of surprise, so, you know, you have shared experiences and certain things that you might feel [are] a little off. If you ask them [whether] they feel it's, like, a little bit odd—like, does this person kind of talk to you a little bit funny? And they're like, yeah.

Like Mitch, for Nathan, the opportunity to have black male colleagues who relate to the challenges that work in the medical profession can bring becomes necessary and important. Significantly, black men's experiences provide a normalizing effect. By virtue of being in the minority, black professional men may wonder whether the issues and challenges they encounter are unique to them. By connecting with other black men who provide social support, they are able to contextualize their experiences with racism, discrimination, and inequality more broadly rather than attributing them to their own perceptions.

Respondents also cited the ability to "be themselves" as one of the advantages of developing close ties to other black men in their professions. Randy, an attorney, says:

Hey, when we go to lunch, our phone voices are shed. It's like, "Whew, I'm tire'; I'm wore out; I've been talking like this all day." Yeah, you let your hair down with your homeboys. Y'all can play; y'all can talk; y'all can chit-chat. You moan, you complain. Then you hit the door; you tighten up: [*changing his voice*] "All right, see y'all later." So, it's solidarity. But it's a good thing.

Randy's impersonation of how basic diction changes when black men are among themselves reveals a core aspect of both the level of solidarity they develop with one another and the extent to which black male workers must still conform to fit into predominantly white male workplaces. Note that he refers to the "phone voices" black men use in their jobs. Using these phone voices (which presumably extend to interactions within the office as well), black men present themselves in a fashion that is likely to be well received by white colleagues. It is only when they are among other black men who, they feel, can relate to and understand these challenges that they drop the phone voices and can comfortably be themselves. This quote highlights that even as black men may face some opportunities to bond with white male colleagues and capitalize on the gendered nature of their occupations, they are still outsiders who have to work in numerous ways to fit into the dominant culture of their organizations and their workplaces.

Still other men talk about the importance of black men helping other black men. Andy, the partnered attorney, describes his efforts to help other lawyers: "I always looked out for the black attorneys because when they came in, there weren't necessarily people doing the same things for them, and I tried to create opportunities or tried to use my influence to get them the opportunities they [others] would have."

As Andy and other attorneys interviewed for this project describe, advancement as an attorney depends heavily on good relationships with partners who are willing to advocate for and support junior associates. Inasmuch as Andy observes that these relationships are not always forged between mostly white partners and the few black attorneys who enter the firm, he attempts to fill these gaps himself by trying to create opportunities for black lawyers that parallel those of their white colleagues.

Randy, the attorney, argues that this willingness to help and assist other black men in the profession is generally widespread:

> I do believe . . . in my heart that black men that get here—dang, you had to work hard to get here. And you didn't get here on your own; somebody had to help you up. And you just owe it to help the next cat. I do believe, genuinely, a lot of brothers do believe that. There's some out there who's out for self. But . . . most of them here understand what it took to get here, so they're willing to help others. They are, they are, yeah. They're willing to help, to a degree.

Here, Randy indicates that black men recognize the challenges they face and how structural and institutional barriers create a different experience for them. This means they are usually willing to "help the next cat." Other research on black workers has shown that gender/ethnic solidarity is not necessarily unusual.[23] However, this kind of solidarity does challenge the theoretical expectation that suggests social pressures lead members of the minority to turn against one another rather than engage and establish support.

Limits to Solidarity: Gender and Class

Although black men do describe a sense of camaraderie and affinity with other black men, they cite some limitations as well. Some respondents argue that while black men generally support one another, they lack the level and depth of support they observe among black professional women. Jack, a partner in a small law firm he co-owns, talks about how he swiftly bonded with black male colleagues:

> When you do meet another black man [lawyer], first of all, you're sort of taken aback, but then you're like, [*in an excited voice*] "What's up?" Hopefully, he'll have the same kind of solidarity. [While at a previous job,] we formed a group—these twelve associates formed an e-mail group—and we would talk about issues. I can't remember what we called it, but it just shows you [we were connected]. [And when I started that job], immediately, as soon as I got hired, a couple days later, one of the black associates walked into my office and was like, "Hey, you need to get hooked up with such and such." So there is definitely some sense of solidarity.

Jack describes this e-mail group (which was made up of black male attorneys in the area) as an example of men's solidarity but then goes on to say:

> I would say when it comes to women in a large law firm, I would imagine they would probably be closer. Because I just feel like men and the experiences that I've had with men in this profession—we're not really about all crying on each other's shoulders. Although we are there to help out if we can, or to bounce ideas off of, I don't know if we're necessarily as close as maybe women are.

Though he acknowledges that he is speculating, Jack's perception is that women are able to have closer ties to one another and develop a deeper level of social support than are black men.

Another attorney makes a similar point. Woody, the lawyer with a large firm, speaks rather wistfully about the differences he sees between black men's and black women's levels of support. He mentions that in previous years, when other black men worked at the firm as associates, he had hoped to develop closer relationships with them. He contrasts this to what happened with the black female attorneys in the firm:

> A year ago, we had eight of us. You know, my mind was, I had this idea that we would get together once a month or so and just do an after-work type thing so we would know each other. Because knowing each other, I think, helps. If I know you, then I'm going to call and check on you every now and then to make sure you're getting the kind of work you need to be getting—whatever. And it just didn't work. No one really saw the benefit of doing that or believed in that. And now all of them are gone. So I wish they had seen a need in it. [In contrast,] we lost some black women, but we didn't lose as many; we lost *all* of the black males except one. We didn't lose that many black females. We still got a couple of them. I think it's because they're looking out for each other. . . . But if we're not talking to each other, and I'm just slow and I'm not getting any work, I'm just going to go home [and] tell my wife that I'm not really doing that much work. And I'm not going to tell anybody, so nobody's going to know that that's the case. I want to be able to talk to somebody and say this is the situation and then, eventually, you know, I'm not going to have billable hours that I need. Or I'm not going to meet the targets I need to meet, and then I'm going to get laid off or pushed out or whatever. (Emphasis in original.)

Though Woody laments the lack of solidarity that occurred among black men when they were employed at his firm, his statement is important because it underscores the very real value that solidarity among members of the minority can have. As he describes, the basic connections to other attorneys in the firm can mean the difference between remaining in the job and being pushed out or fired. When black men do not have these connections, and they are already in jobs where they are in the numerical minority, the consequences can be dire.

Essentially, Jack and Woody argue that gendered behavior serves to limit the levels of solidarity that black men develop in these professions. When they contrast black men's solidarity to black women's, they generally contend that the "feminine" characteristic of being more supportive and compassionate helps them to create strong relationships. These relationships assist them in jobs, where not only are they in the numerical minority but (as many men have stated) they face even greater challenges because of the masculine character of these professions. These men assert that solidarity is important and welcomed among black male professionals, but at the same time, the behaviors that are associated with masculinity—unwillingness to be too vulnerable, approachable, or helpful—work to black men's disadvantage because these behaviors preclude them from developing the sort of close relationships that could help them combat the challenges they encounter in the workplace.

Several respondents also cite class differences as a factor that limited solidarity. Interestingly, these men highlight how their positions in professional occupations create greater challenges in their interactions with and sense of connection to black men who do not share their income and status level. Thus, while black professional men are less likely to turn against other colleagues as a means of currying favor with members of the dominant group, there are many cases in which the processes of upward mobility and advancement serve to minimize any sense of solidarity they may feel with black men en masse.

Mitch, the emergency room doctor, provides a particularly eloquent example of this challenge. He is from a working-class family in the Northeast and is the only member of his family to advance to a comfortably upper-middle-class lifestyle. Here, he describes some of the contradictions and challenges that accompany that upward mobility:

> I have friends that I would love to go and hang out with. I can't do it anymore because of what they do. I know even if I just go and see some of my friends, just because of the situations that they're in and what they do on a regular basis, I could put my whole career in jeopardy, my whole family, my life in jeopardy,

and things like that. And a lot of us go through that. Not just physicians but successful black people in general. When you leave the neighborhood and you come back with a college education or you go off to college, it's, "Oh, you're not the same person anymore." No, I'm not the same person anymore because I can't hang out on the corner with you and talk shit because if the cops come by and we all get arrested and I get arrested, I can't be out here with you because you're selling drugs. I'm not doing that. That's not going to happen.

Mitch makes clear that the challenges of developing a level of solidarity with black men are, in his case, much more class than race based. Note that earlier he discusses how he values being able to bond and interact with the two other black male emergency room doctors in the hospital where he works and appreciates the support and encouragement he receives from them. In contrast, his upward mobility threatens his ties to former friends and associates, making cross-class interaction with black men much more difficult and complicated than before.

Andy, the law-firm partner, also talks about the difficulty of maintaining cross-class ties with other black men:

I don't have the same interests as my cousins. I belong to the One Twelve Society, or I go to breakfast, and everybody's wearing a suit, and you get waited on hand and foot. Not that there's a resentment or anything, but you know. I'll give you an example. A good friend of mine, when we were real young, we lost contact, and I saw him probably when I was about twenty-four, and I said, "Hey, how are you? Good to see you." And he said, "Man, talk to me regular." And I was sort of like okay, whatever. And he said, "Well, what are you doing now?" "Well, I'm in law school, and I graduated from Marquette." [He replied,] "About time you graduated." But I graduated from engineering school in four years, which takes most people five, but whatever. I didn't say that to him, but I'm thinking that in my mind.

Like Mitch, Andy describes his background as primarily working class. Yet advancing to a partnership position with a prestigious law firm creates some challenges in his ability to remain connected to his working-class roots. He demonstrates this in contrasting himself to cousins who do not belong to elite clubs or have the same social experiences that he does and also in how he highlights the different paths (and reactions to these paths) from his childhood friend. And like Mitch, Andy speaks candidly about the importance of forming ties to other black men in his profession. Ultimately, however, the class differences produced by upward mobility mean that this sort of solidarity can be limited to men who share the same occupational status.

Teddy, the engineer, also addresses this issue. In describing the extent to which he felt solidarity with another black man who briefly worked for his company, he says:

> It was kind of cool [having another black man there]. [Sometimes] you want to talk about collard greens or pork chops, neck bones, or something like that. It's kind of cool. [But that's] if you can find people that are truly my contemporaries, that have similar backgrounds. But if you [mean] talk to folks [who are] still thugging, still clubbing—that kind of thing—then, yeah, I don't enjoy that. Because, it's, well, . . . I don't enjoy that; let's leave it at that. If it's something that I just believe is just foolishness, then I just prefer not to be around that. That's just not something I generally approve of. It's just something that I believe—sounds weird to say, but—holds us back as a people, that kind of behavior. And I'm just not comfortable being around it.

During the interview, it was clear Teddy was being a bit sarcastic when he said he sometimes wants to discuss collard greens, pork chops, and neck bones. By referencing foods that are commonly associated with soul food and black American culture, he alludes to how working with another black male can be a positive thing that evokes familiarity and cultural similarity. However, he subtly introduces a very particularized dynamic to this: he conveys that he is more comfortable associating with certain types of black people—specifically, those who embrace the middle-class values that he appreciates. Other black people who are still "thugging and clubbing" and engaging in behaviors attributed to lower- and working-class blacks are considered less appealing.

The responses these men give reveal a complex, nuanced picture of the extent and limits of black men's solidarity with other black men. As members of a numerical minority, theoretically, we might expect them to turn against one another and to try to distance themselves from other black men to gain acceptance from the dominant group. Yet this is not what occurs. Black men describe feeling a core connection with other black men in their professions. They rely on one another to cope with racial incidents and problems in the workplace, and they also look to one another to reflect the realities of their experiences as men in the racial minority. At the same time, however, the processes that push black professional men to connect with one another also exacerbate the difficulties they face in maintaining ties to black men outside of their class and social status. As one of few black male doctors in the hospital or engineers in the firm, black men see other black men in these jobs as people who truly understand their experiences. Simultaneously, they become less connected to black men who do not share their class position as a function of lifestyle and social and economic differences. Further, in several cases, they identify how gendered behaviors associated with masculinity limit black men's ability to form ties that could go even further in enhancing their occupational ascension. Partial tokenization keeps these black professionals from turning on one another, but they still fail to develop solidarity to the fullest extent possible.

Summary

In this chapter, I consider how partial tokenization shapes black men's relationships and interactions with other men. The theory of tokenism suggests that as members of the numerical minority, these men find dominant groups use various tools—exaggerating differences and interrupting, for example—to highlight the perceived contrasts between themselves and the tokens. Further, according to the theory, this contrasting puts distance between themselves and other black men to show white males in the dominant group that they are loyal, can fit in, and can be trusted.

However, the results of this study suggest a more complicated process. Black professional men are aware of contrasts between themselves and dominant group members. However, these contrasts are rarely established through white male coworkers' and supervisors' overt and intentional efforts. A key factor that establishes the contrasts between black men and their white male colleagues is differential access to social networks. Black men are very conscious of the fact that white men tend to come to professional jobs equipped with the social ties and relationships that enable them to hit the ground running, whereas black men must work long and hard to develop these sorts of connections. At the same time, working in gendered occupations affords men the opportunity to link up with mentors who can facilitate their career advancement. In these "masculine" professions, black men have various means by which they take advantage of gendered norms, behaviors, and structures that enable them to advance in their careers. Thus, intersections of race and gender leave these men less equipped with social networks than their white male peers, while at the same time rendering them able to offset this disadvantage by developing ties to well-connected white male elites.

When it comes to interactions with other black men, the theory of partial tokenization also offers a more precise framework. Unlike the tokens Rosabeth Moss Kanter describes, black men do not turn from other black men in an effort to connect with white male dominants.[24] Instead, they recognize their own experiences in those of other black men in their professions, and this creates a feeling of solidarity and camaraderie among them. Indeed, black men describe sharing a special bond with other black male colleagues—they can openly discuss the vagaries and challenges that make being a black professional male unique. As many respondents suggest, other black professional men are the only ones who truly understand their experiences. Thus, intersections of race, class, and gender influence how black men bond with others in their profession. Given that black men encounter particular experiences shaped by these intersecting factors, it makes sense that they would feel a sense of kinship with others whom they expect can relate to the issues they face.

However, the limits of their solidarity also reflect intersections of race, gender, and—particularly—class. Even though black men speak strongly about the importance of connecting with other black men, they also concede that gendered perceptions of masculinity preclude them from developing this solidarity to its fullest. Because they do not have women's "natural" empathy and concern, they are unable to offer each other support that could serve as more of a buffer against the racialized challenges that often imperil black workers in professional environments. Race and gender thus intersect to allow black professional men to develop and appreciate ties to one another, but they do not necessarily carry this solidarity to its logical conclusion.

Additionally, intersections of race and class shape the ways in which black men feel solidarity for other black men outside of their profession, class, and/or status group. While other black professional men are perceived to "get it" and understand these men's challenges, the process of upward mobility has deleterious effects for the relationships between these men and their working-class or working-poor counterparts. Even—or perhaps especially—for black men who were raised working class, the specific challenges and privileges associated with an upper-middle-class lifestyle render them noticeably different from their working-class peers and inhibit the extent to which the solidarity they feel for other black men can cross class boundaries. The experience of partial tokenization means that intersecting factors—race, gender, and class—shape the appreciation for and pursuit of solidarity between professional black men, but these factors simultaneously work to constrain this sense of connectedness.

This has implications for these black men as members of the middle class. For many years, research on the black middle class has shown the existence of cross-class tension between these blacks and their lower- and working-class counterparts.[25] Inasmuch as black men interviewed for this study have a sense of an eroding connection to black men in the lower class, their ties to those in the upper classes are strengthened. In other words, partial tokenization allows black men to form relatively easy gender ties to their white male colleagues to the extent that they may actually feel more of a sense of commonality with white men of a similar status than black men in the working class.

5 | Black Men and Masculinity

The last two chapters have examined the ways partial tokenization shapes black professional men's interactions with white and black women and men in the workplace. Given the male-dominated, gendered occupations in which these men are employed, it is also important to assess how the gendered character of their jobs influences their sense of masculinity in the workplace. Other studies of male-dominated positions in the legal, construction, and financial industries assert that men's display of certain attributes of masculinity—decisiveness, aggressiveness, and a willingness to take risks, for example—is an important, if intangible, aspect of job performance.[1] Other researchers, however, have shown that intersections of race and gender can impede the ways men of color are free to exhibit some of these "masculine" traits.[2] In this chapter, I examine black male workers' encounters with images of black masculinity in the workplace. Further, I analyze the role partial tokenization plays in enabling them to construct alternate representations that challenge these depictions of masculinity.

Assimilation and Informal Roles

In previous chapters, I discuss black men's encounters with two of the three perceptual tendencies Rosabeth Moss Kanter attributes to tokens.[3]

One tendency is heightened visibility. The other is the contrasts established between black professional men and members of the dominant
group. In this section, I examine how black men face issues with assimilation, the third perceptual tendency Kanter identifies.[4]

Kanter asserts that as a consequence of being in the numerical minority, "tokens can never really be seen as they are, and they are always
fighting stereotypes. The characteristics of tokens as individuals are often distorted to fit preexisting generalizations about their category as a
group."[5] In other words, when certain groups are members of the minority, it becomes easier for those in the majority to evaluate and interact
with them based on stereotypes and preconceived notions, rather than
get to know them as individuals. Additionally—and more problematic
for those in the minority—the use of stereotypes allows those in the
dominant group to relegate tokens to roles, behaviors, and expectations
that limit their abilities to excel and flourish in the organization.

Kanter describes several processes by which issues related to assimilation create problems for those in the numerical minority.[6] She
contends that the efforts and challenges associated with assimilation
generally lead to *role encapsulation*, wherein the token is trapped by the
role for which he or she is seen to be a "natural" fit. Processes that facilitate this include *mistaken identity* and *status leveling*. With mistaken
identity, tokens are erroneously perceived as filling a role specifically tai-
lored to members of their group, and they are seen to fit this role more
perfectly than they fit into the organization as a whole. Status leveling
reinforces the idea that the token belongs specifically in this initial role
rather than belonging as a fully functioning member of the group.

In Kanter's analysis, this applies clearly to the women who are part
of the corporation.[7] For instance, women executives in the organization
face mistaken identity when they are assumed to be secretaries, assis-
tants, wives, or dates rather than high-ranking employees within the
firm. While these misperceptions can be corrected—though that also
requires time, energy, and possibly stress—status leveling is more pernicious. This occurs for women executives when, despite establishing their
roles and positions in the organization, they are responded to in terms
of their gender rather than their occupational status. Thus, in meetings,
women executives may be expected to take the minutes, thereby filling a secretarial role. In both cases, it is easier to "fit the token woman

to [men's] preexisting generalizations about women than to change the category."[8]

One of the key mechanisms through which both of these processes occur involves the informal roles to which women are subjected. Members of the dominant group are likely to see numerical minorities as people who fill particular slots or embody "stereotyped informal roles." These are roles tokens are expected to fit based largely on generalized assumptions about their behaviors, skills, and attitudes. As Kanter writes, "Dominants can incorporate tokens and still preserve their generalizations by inducting tokens into stereotypical roles that preserve familiar forms of interaction between the kinds of people represented by the token and the dominants."[9] These roles allow members of the dominant group to cast those in the numerical minority in recognizable roles, regardless of whether they truly fit the minority group member.

For women in the organization, Kanter argues that four informal roles predominate.[10] Women are cast as the mother, the seductress, the pet, or the iron maiden (see Table 5.1). These roles grow out of the fact that men, as members of the dominant group, see women in ways that are directly related to their sexuality. Thus, women face a Madonna/whore dynamic vis-à-vis the respective mother and seductress roles. Alternatively, they can become desexualized or hypersexualized in the pet or the iron maiden role. These roles offer men a way to interact with and relate to the women in their midst. Ultimately, however, the roles are based largely on stereotypical ideas about gender and femininity and can become confining and restrictive for women by concealing their capabilities, skills, and competency.

Kanter contends that several responses to the challenges of assimilation ensue.[11] Some tokens may accept the roles in which they are cast. For instance, some women may relish how their gender enables them to interact with male colleagues in ways that are generally forbidden, or at least frowned upon. In their study of gender and sexism in contemporary society, Nijole Benokraitis and Joe Feagin cite a female college administrator who asserts that her gender enables her to soothe tensions and conflicts between men, much like the mother role that Kanter describes: "When I was on the faculty, I purposely negotiated between the faculty, especially the men, who are always squabbling. . . . I'd comfort the losers and praise the winners. . . . I made sure, too, that I never

TABLE 5.1   WOMEN'S INFORMAL ROLES

Role	Characteristics
Mother	Seen as nurturing, caring, "easy to talk to"; identified with emotional matters; seen as safe, desexualized.
Seductress	Seen as sex object, sometimes "protected" by a high-profile male ally; seen as sexually attractive, obscuring other attributes.
Pet	Seen as a mascot, an observer; not expected to perform at a man's level; seen as minimally competent, preventing equal-status contact.
Iron maiden	Seen as extremely tough, brittle, possibly militant; refusing behaviors that could cast her in the other roles, she is considered "difficult" and possibly "dangerous"; rarely finds sympathy or protection from male colleagues.

Based on data from Rosabeth Moss Kanter, *Men and Women of the Corporation* (New York: Basic Books, 1997).

aligned myself with the feminist faculty. . . . Giving a lot of small, classy parties didn't hurt."[12]

Women may resign themselves to adopting one of the four informal stereotypes, while still others may choose to interact primarily or even exclusively with known others to avoid the mistaken identity and status leveling that could accompany interactions with new colleagues. Some women work hard to challenge any and all stereotypes that come their way, while others allow male allies to "protect" them the best they can from these informal dynamics. Regardless of the strategy chosen, coping with these stereotypes, informal roles, and generalizations prove particularly taxing to women workers. And ultimately, the existence of these stereotypes (whether women fight them or embrace them) reinforces their power and "confirms dominants' stereotypes, [proving] to them how right they were all along."[13]

Black Men's Informal Roles

The informal roles Kanter observes in her study of the corporation are clearly shaped by gender, reflecting the dominant group's stereotypes about femininity and sexuality.[14] Consequently, these roles do not necessarily offer a template for examining the ways that black professional men confront informal roles—black men in a male-dominated occupation are probably unlikely to be cast as seductresses or mothers. Yet informal roles are certainly present for black men. Many respondents talked often about being stereotyped by colleagues, customers, and others in the work environment. The informal roles they encounter, however, are grounded in stereotypes that reflect intersections of race, gender, and masculinity. Representations based on these criteria are prepackaged so as to be immediately familiar to members of the dominant group. As such, I argue that black professional men face three stereotyped informal roles—the "superbrother," the "impostor," and the "race representative"—that affect their occupational experiences and impede their ability to assimilate into the dominant group.

The Superbrother

Several respondents describe facing the image of the superbrother, who they characterize as an archetypal black male worker with excellent credentials, a stellar educational background, and virtually no professional flaws whatsoever. In the words of several respondents, the superbrothers are "the best of the best." They attended elite universities, have experience working with the top judges or in the top firms, and can boast of nearly incomparable résumés. Yet, as many respondents point out, superbrothers not only are few and far between but are held to standards that are rarely if ever expected of white male colleagues. The informal role of the superbrother thus sets up a nearly impossible-to-achieve example that most black men in the organization are nonetheless expected to reach. This places higher standards on black professional men in many ways—they are expected to be better educated, trained, and experienced than their white male counterparts, who face advantages in the educational arenas that precede employment.[15]

The lawyer Randy was the first respondent to bring this informal role to my attention and the one who coined the "superbrother" term:

> I thought about this six or seven years ago, when I was at my first big firm. And every black man that was at that firm had either graduated from a top twenty law school, had a law review with a moot court, or had clerked for a federal judge. There were only six or seven of us. We were all elite, so to speak. But we were surrounded by average white guys. I had to be—every brother in that firm had to be—a rock star. He had to be the best of the best. But I could sit next door to this guy who had graduated

middle of the pack from University of Georgia. Or I could go to lunch with another white guy who had graduated from Mercer, kind of like middle of the pack. And I would always wonder, "Well, how can I be the average?" or "Why do I always have to be the best of the best?" All the brothers went to lunch one day. This is when I was leaving; this is when I thought about it. One of the guys had graduated from Morehouse [and] from Yale Law. I had graduated from Tulane. I had clerked for a federal judge. My other buddy had graduated from University of Virginia, and then the other brother, I mean, we were just like [*gesturing to indicate they were at the top*]. And we all had kind of gotten on the elevator at the same time with another group of our counterparts, white cats, and they had all graduated from Florida, Georgia, and I'm like, it doesn't match. It just doesn't match. I actually told the head of professional development there—I said, "Y'all couldn't fill an entire law firm with the credentials that you force the black guys to have." You couldn't fill a—you'd have fifty of us and that's it; you'd have fifty total.

As Randy eloquently describes, the bar is so much higher for black male attorneys that it would be nearly impossible for firms to hire too many of them. Nonetheless, this is the informal standard against which many black men feel they are measured.

Attorney Jack observes the same phenomena in practice. He discusses the influence law school rank has on hiring for black men:

At your midsize law firm or at your small law firm, . . . you got so many good old boys and good old girls who come there with Georgia State law degrees, and—I don't know where you went, sorry—we're talking Georgia State law degrees. But talking about what a black man has to do to get in the door as opposed to anybody else, I would say about 80 percent [of white students attended a state school]. I remember a [white] Notre Dame graduate and a UCLA graduate. UCLA is pretty good, but by far the majority [were from] Georgia State in Georgia [with] a couple of Emorys in there. But to even break in [as a black man], you had to go to a Georgetown. You had to have these kinds of accolades to even get in the door.

As Jack notes, he observes a sharp contrast between the educational backgrounds of his white peers and those of black male attorneys. He goes on to describe the implications of this when it comes to hiring:

> You got people going to schools that aren't [ranked] where the Harvards and your Yales and your Georgetowns are. But those people will make it in like that. And they are not graduating magna cum laude, but they're in. I just know from my perspective, a lot of my brothers and sisters—they got a deal. I wish I could've avoided this hundred-thousand-dollar loan payment that I have to pay back and just went to the average Joe law school, but . . . There is a school—I think it's called John Marshall Law school. I've seen plenty of white guys from there [working at major firms], but I haven't seen any brothers; I'll put it like that. I haven't seen too many brothers going to John Marshall being at these large law firms, but I have seen white people from those schools. I think that's the best way to say it.

Jack makes a particularly insightful argument about the consequences of the superbrother role. The fallout from this role creates not only false and possibly unrealistic expectations for employers but also additional financial burdens for the black men who are subjected to it. As Jack points out, his $100,000 law school debt that has secured him a high-level law degree likewise secures his employability. Yet white male (and female) peers who are employable with the "average Joe" law school degree are able to avoid thousands of dollars worth of debt. Given the research that indicates racial wealth disparities are a particularly pernicious form of contemporary inequality—and that these wealth disparities are often exacerbated by educational attainment—Jack's statements highlight how these informal roles can have far-reaching consequences.[16]

The Impostor

A second stereotyped informal role that black men face is the impostor. This role is grounded in stereotypes and representations of black men as ill-suited for high-ranking, high-status occupations. Many respondents report that they are, consequently, subjected to this informal role when they interact with other workers in the organization—including colleagues—who mistake them for lower-status individuals and attempt to treat them as such. The impostor role, then, surfaces when black men are treated as people who do not *really* belong in medicine, engineering, law, or finance but are deemed better suited for other work.

George, the engineering professor at a major research university, describes the way he first encountered this impostor role at his workplace, speaking in terms of the racial dynamics present in the larger society:

> When I first arrived here, there were the people that weren't— how do I put this correctly? I was mistaken for a technician when I was in the copy room. Someone thought I was fixing the copy machine, but you know, that is not always because the person is not an enlightened person. It may also be a symptom of society where they see people in certain stereotyped roles and are not used to seeing people of color in this type of role. [These things] are no different than anywhere else in the U.S. in this period of time. The same sorts of things happen when I go to the mall and get followed or if a woman rolls up a window when I walk by. It's the same situation. So [my job] is not unusual with those types of things.

George notes that the stereotyped informal role of the impostor is grounded largely in perceptions that black men are typically relegated to working-class, lower-status occupations. His job as a professor makes him a bit of a standout in this regard. However, colleagues operating under the assumption that black men work in low-skill jobs rather than as research professors still force him to confront and cope with this particular stereotyped informal role.

Jared, another engineering professor, shares several stories of his encounters with the impostor role. In various cases, he describes being mistaken for a campus visitor who is illegally parking in the faculty lot, a staff member who erroneously selects a form intended for faculty, and a female student's brother rather than her graduate faculty adviser. In each case, Jared describes other members of the campus community who first fail to realize that he is a faculty member and then express surprise that he is employed in that capacity. Here, Jared recounts the story of being mistaken for his student's brother:

I went with her when her petition was to be heard, and we waited outside the room where the hearings would take place. They opened the door to let her in—and, I presumed, me in as her adviser. So, the door opened, and she walked in—she was in front of me. And then the guy who was the secretary, he said, "You can't come in." That's all he said. "You can't come in," and he closed the door. That puzzled me. I said, wouldn't an adviser [be allowed in]? But the door stayed closed for maybe five or ten seconds and then opened again, and he said, "Oh, you can come in. I thought you were her brother." And then it was, "You look so young." And maybe I did look young. But the thing about it is that the young lady and I did not look anything alike. Not that we couldn't have been brother and sister, but again, it's a presumption. Rather than ask me, "Oh, why are you here?" it's just automatic. Well, you know, *you* couldn't possibly be a faculty member, so we're not—that's not even in the consciousness. So that was just what you might call a prejudice where, black—black brother, not professor. (Emphasis in original.)

As Jared describes, the immediate presumption is that he is a peer of this graduate student, rather than someone who actually occupies a position of higher status than the secretary who questions him. Even though the hearing he describes is one in which a faculty adviser (and not a sibling) would likely accompany a student, a member of the dominant group (ironically, one of lower status) relies on stereotypes to assess where Jared likely fits in the organizational hierarchy. Significantly, in acting on these stereotypes, the first role to which Jared is assigned is that of the impostor. He is immediately seen as someone who does not fit the position he has earned and actually occupies. As he puts it, the possibility that he might genuinely fit the role of the faculty member rather than a more stereotypical one is "not even in the consciousness."

Other respondents share that this informal role can take on a more menacing tone. They describe cases in which they are literally perceived not only as impostors but also as people who pose a threat to colleagues or to the organization at large. Woody, the attorney, recounts one such example:

I was coming off of the elevator, and this female partner, who's on my floor—who's freaking two doors down from me—was getting off the elevator. I allowed her to get off the elevator first, which I always do, and I was coming behind her to get in the door on our floor, and she waved her badge and she *literally* tried to close the door to keep me from getting in. And I had to show her my badge, like with my picture on it that [shows] I work here, for her to let me in. . . . First of all, I had on a suit. I didn't have a tie on, but I had on a suit. I mean, what do you think I am? Let's assume you thought I was a copy guy; still, why are you—she's acting like a—she's literally closing the door! Maybe she thought I was going to hurt her. I don't know what she was thinking. But that kind of stuff, those types of things happen, and you have to be mindful. Every day, I have to think, okay, well, how's this person perceiving me? They haven't seen me in court. They haven't seen any of the briefs that I've written. They haven't seen me interact with a client. So they don't know my abilities as a lawyer. All they see is the black bald guy who, if he was stuck in traffic that morning, has an angry face or—so I don't know what it's going to be. So those types of things make it uniquely hard for black men. And so then when you don't have people that look like you who've been around for a while, [but] they know that white men are lawyers, it's kind of hard.

Here, Woody eloquently describes the ways that dominant groups rely on stereotypes to understand those in the numerical minority, typically to their disadvantage. As he points out, white colleagues are not able to "see" his qualifications, and relying on the stereotyped informal role of the impostor means they rarely assume that he is a trained lawyer who has written many briefs, has good relationships with clients, and is proficient at his job. They do, however, see his race and gender. And as he insightfully notes, in the absence of large numbers of other black men in this field, it is easier for those in the racial majority to use the abundant stereotypes of black male criminality and threat to shape their interactions with him.

Additionally, Woody's case highlights some of the particulars of how stereotyped informal roles may shape black men's occupational experiences differently from their black female peers. For black men, this issue of being perceived as threatening and dangerous is a nearly constant underlying aspect of how they navigate the workplace. Note that Woody guesses that the white female partner in the exchange above may have feared that he would cause her harm. This is a particularly racialized and gendered manifestation of the challenges black men face as a result of being in the numerical minority and one that can profoundly affect the stereotyped informal role of the impostor. As this example and several of the following ones reveal, the raced, gendered cultural image of black men as dangerous people can mean that black men are not just taken to be impostors but ones who pose a threat.

Kurtis offers an example that reinforces this as well. He too shares several stories of having to confront people who attempt to cast him as an impostor. In his interview, he describes showing up early for a lecture only to be mistaken for a custodian as well as going unrecognized by staff and colleagues alike. Here, he discloses a particularly damaging case of being treated as an impostor:

> I was a chief resident at the university, and—this is actually one of my most painful memories of just being a physician, period. Some fellow is at the hospital impersonating a doctor, stealing supplies at a local hospital. Now I've been at that program for three years. I've been in everybody's face the whole time. If you're the chief resident, obviously, you're kind of the smartest guy, and so you're doing the consults; you're pressing the flesh with other doctors. A secretary of the chief of medicine got it in her head that I was the guy who was the impostor. This is a true story—that I must have been that person stealing because she hadn't seen this black doctor before. So I came out of an attending's room one day, and there's like thirty people outside, and I just looked. I thought someone had had a heart attack or something. But the funny thing is they were actually looking at me because this woman was like, "That's the guy." And people went, "Are you crazy? That's Dr. Williams. He's coming out of the chief resident's room." She said, "No, I saw him; he's here late." This is a real story. So I went over to her and said, "You know the funny thing is I've been doing the consults for three

years, but you've never looked at my face, which is okay. I'm invisible to you, and that's not a big issue with me. But let me explain what is. I am going to talk to your boss and tell him how I feel about this."

Kurtis goes on to describe the response he got when he informed the chief of medicine about the accusations leveled against him:

> And I did, and I said it was reprehensible. I called my chairman, and the chairman chewed them all out. The interesting thing is some of the other attendings in the university—the dermatology attendings who were doing slides—they said, "Oh man, did you hear this hilarious story that happened to Kurtis? It was hilarious." And it wasn't hilarious, man. I mean, I am a black person up here with just one other black person, the chairman, and I got accused of being an impostor thief physician stealing supplies. That's not funny.

Fortunately for Kurtis, his supervisor happened to be another black male who likely understood and perhaps personally appreciated the gravity of the accusations leveled against him. At any rate, Kurtis presents a stark example of being treated as an impostor, again initiated by someone who, ironically, occupied a lower status position in the organizational hierarchy than he did.

Once again, the presumption of threat depends on exactly how some respondents are cast in the impostor role. While George and Jared suffer stereotyping as people who could not possibly fit the roles they actually occupy, Woody's and Kurtis's experiences make clear that being defined as an impostor can carry with it implicit assumptions that they are dangerous to the social order. This underscores the ways that this informal role is shaped by stereotypes about race, gender, and masculinity—in particular, the idea that black men represent a threat. The image of black men (and black masculinity more broadly) has been used to denote danger and a sense of menace for centuries, and as these men's experiences show, continues to shape informal social roles in which they are cast.

Mitch, the emergency room doctor, makes note of this during his interview. His comments about black men's experiences in the workplace differing from black women's highlight the salience of race and gender stereotypes in shaping the informal roles black men encounter:

> Maybe because we get such a bad reputation in the general media that it's always hard for—I think it's more of a shock for people to see you [as a black man] coming than it is for a black woman. You don't see black women on TV getting arrested for murder, for drug trafficking, and gang violence, and things like that as much. Even in the black community, [there are] expectations for black women being more successful and—maybe not more successful but more prone to be in a position where they have the opportunity to be more successful than a black man. [As a black man,] you're expected—I think that it's more that you're expected to have trouble or to have problems with authority and problems with the legal system and so forth. So when you see a black man that's made it through all that to a position of success, people are just amazed. And still, they don't really know if you've earned where you got to be. You know, if you got into medical school because of affirmative action, and did he really deserve to be there?

As Mitch notes, these cultural representations—both in popular and news media—of black men as people who are associated with criminality, violence, and other unsavory behaviors influence how they are treated in the workplace. For many of the respondents in this study, these images may affect white coworkers' perceptions of black men in general. Indeed, numerous research studies indicate that whites often maintain derogatory stereotypes of black men, perceiving them as prone to violence.[17] Given this, it is perhaps not surprising that black male professionals may feel that white colleagues view them through this lens and, on seeing them in professional roles, attempt to recast them as impostors.

The Race Representative

The third informal role in which black men sometimes find themselves cast is that of the race representative. In this role, they are called on whenever the firm or office needs to show diversity or present someone who is a member of a minority group. The work that men actually do in these contexts is less important than the fact that they are present to underscore the message the organization wants to send about minority representation. Furthermore, being cast as the race representative may cause men's job duties to suffer, as the time and energy associated with this additional work may undermine the ability to complete tasks that are required for advancement or promotion. Randy, the attorney, talks about his experience being cast as the race representative while working at his previous firm:

> I used to go speak at schools for career day. They need somebody black to go to a black school in Fulton? [Then it's] "Hey, Randy." And I'll go do it. Or a lot of the companies here in town—Coke, Bell South, Home Depot—when they need people to do their [legal] work and a team of people [to] come and pitch that work—when a team of lawyers walks in that door, there better be somebody black. So, "Hey, Randy, uh, we need you to go with us to go pitch this." [I'll reply,] "Oh, the other black guy out today?" I jokingly say it, but it's true.

As Randy attests, whenever there is a need for the company to show that they have black attorneys on staff, he is cast in the role of the race representative.

Michael, the engineering professor in his late twenties, also speaks to his experiences facing this role. He describes it as "cultural taxation":

> "We need you to be on this committee because you're an African American." "We need you to go out to dinner because you're an African American." "You should be advised of this because you're an African American." "Could you go participate in this because you're an African American?" You don't have to do any of that crap. If it was important to them, they'd go do it. Don't do anything, or if you'd like to do that, make sure that you get it construed that you get credit for it.

Like Randy, Michael explains that being a *black* engineer means being cast as the race representative, which involves additional, race-related labor. Unlike other colleagues who can simply perform their professional duties, he is expected to take on this extra task because it benefits the university to offer diverse representations of its faculty. Pointedly, Michael notes that these obligations are not terribly important or critical, or they would be done by other faculty or administrators. However, he is nevertheless cast in the role of the race representative when he is expected to complete these tasks as one of few black members of the faculty.

Woody, a patent attorney, speaks with a marked sense of frustration about the added expectations that are placed on him as a black lawyer:

> There's a big company that we've been trying to get business from for a while and haven't been able to do that as a company. It's a pharmaceutical company, and I'm a computer person, so I know diddly-squat about pharmaceuticals. But that company has a mentoring program for diversity kids (i.e., black kids), and so they wanted—the company doesn't have any black in-house lawyers, so they went to the law firms asking for black in-house lawyers. So they came to us, and they told them, "Oh, you got one," so I ended up spending time doing that—which is not billable. So I had to spend time doing that on top of trying to make my billable hours. That's an extra job. Nobody's saying, "Okay, by the way, for being our token black attorney this year, you get an extra $20,000." That ain't going to happen. In fact, I can do all of that, and if I don't make my billable hours, I'm not getting anything. I'm getting demoted—even though I've been spending time doing this sort of stuff. I mean, this is ridiculous. That's two days out of my life that the clock doesn't stop. I have to do e-mails for work. There's things that I'm expected to be able to have done, and at the same time, I have to go. And the only reason why I'm—the *only* reason why I'm here is because I'm black. (Emphasis in original.)

Woody astutely identifies the financial costs to being cast as the race representative. As he points out, the work he does on his "black trip" is not financially compensated or rewarded; in fact, it detracts from the job he is supposed to be doing. Yet it serves the firm to highlight its sole black male associate in certain capacities, even if it does not at all work to Woody's benefit.

When faced with the expectation that they will speak to minority groups and function as the organization's face of color, black professional men are cast in the third informal role as the race representative. In their role as the race representative, these men do labor that is uncompensated and unrewarded but that perhaps is seen as "natural" or "basic" for them because it involves emphasizing their racial status. In some ways, this is similar to the racialized labor that Sharon Collins identifies among black executives. She argues that they are shunted into community outreach and diversity jobs that offer them middle-class salaries but little opportunity for advancement or mobility within the organization.[18] The respondents in my study do not work in the same sorts of jobs that Collins focuses on, but being cast as the race representative subjects them to additional, unpaid labor that can benefit the organization at their financial or occupational expense.[19]

Developing Marginalized Masculinities: A Response to Informal Roles

In professional workplaces, black men have few avenues available for reacting to the informal roles in which members of the dominant group place them. Indeed, as Kanter writes, those in the numerical minority tend to react to the difficulties of assimilation in one of the following ways: they embrace or resignedly accept the roles they are cast in, they challenge the roles openly (which often leads to being cast in new stereotyped informal roles), they seek protection from members of the dominant group, or they stand alone.[20] Few, if any, of the respondents in my study follow these pathways. Instead, they adopt certain kinds of masculine behavior as strategies to avoid the informal roles they are assigned while still performing their jobs effectively. Once again, the concept of partial tokenization appears to fit black professional men's experiences in these jobs more precisely. They experience some aspects of tokenization, which constrains their ability to assimilate into mostly white workplaces. However, intersections of race and gender permit them to employ certain tropes of masculinity so that, at times, they can sidestep their informal roles and reconstruct themselves as men within a largely masculinized environment.

The theory of hegemonic masculinity provides a useful theoretical framework for contextualizing the ways black professional men develop certain masculinities that help them navigate the work environment. Developed by Raewyn Connell, the theory of hegemonic masculinity argues that masculinities are relational and connected.[21] In other words, rather than contending that *all* men have the same advantages over *all* women, there are various types of masculinities that exist in societies. The hegemonic version is the normalized image of masculinity that is held up as the ideal. In contemporary society, hegemonic masculinity praises risk taking, status, physical prowess, stoicism, rationality, and, perhaps most significantly, the superiority of masculinity.[22] As sociologist Erving Goffman wrote long ago, it also tacitly includes being white, heterosexual, wealthy, male, and of American nationality:

> In an important sense there is only one complete unblushing male in America: a young, married, white, urban, northern, heterosexual, Protestant father of good education, fully employed, of good complexion, weight, and height, and a recent record in sports. Every American male tends to look out upon the world from this perspective. . . . Any male who fails to qualify in any one of these ways is likely to view himself—during moments at least—as unworthy, incomplete, and inferior.[23]

Hegemonic masculinity is also historical and thus changes depending on the social and material conditions of the time. Therefore, hegemonic masculinity of the Puritan age emphasized asceticism and religious faith more so than the hegemonic masculinity of contemporary U.S. society.[24]

With a definition of hegemonic masculinity, it is possible to assess where other masculinities stand in relation to it. As Goffman notes, most men do not achieve hegemonic masculinity, though it is held up as an ideal to which all men should strive and some men will attempt to reach it. Connell categorizes this as "complicit" masculinity and describes it as a form of masculinity that occurs when men struggle to achieve the hegemonic ideal and police others according to its dictates.[25]

In his study of young, mostly white middle-class American men, sociologist Michael Kimmel finds numerous examples of these men engaging in a complicit masculinity. They relentlessly monitor themselves and other men for deviations from the hegemonic ideal.[26]

Hegemonic and complicit masculinities exist in opposition to the subordinated masculinities typically associated with gay men. These displays of masculine behavior provide the relief against which hegemonic and complicit masculinities define themselves. If subordinated masculinity is associated with gay men and is represented as behavior that is effete, emotional, and dangerously close to the feminine, then this reinforces the idea that hegemonic masculinity is rational, dominant, strong, and powerful. Hegemonic masculinity therefore presumably provides a sharp contrast to subordinated masculinity. In her study of the ways that "fag" imagery is used among high school boys, C. J. Pascoe offers a clear example of how this type of subordinate masculinity is used as a contrast to the more valued hegemonic ideal.[27]

Finally, Connell also acknowledges the existence of marginalized masculinities.[28] These reflect masculinities that have been pushed to the side and are typically associated with socially disadvantaged groups. Thus, the masculinity associated with working-class men might be considered a marginalized masculinity, as is the masculinity associated with different racial and ethnic groups. It is here that Connell brings race into play and considers how it can intersect with gender to create performances of masculinity that may be different from—albeit informed by—the hegemonic ideal.[29]

Other studies have taken this analysis further to show how men of color may perform marginalized masculinities that either strive to approximate or establish differences from the hegemonic ideal. In his study of Chinese American men, Anthony Chen argues that these men are likely to strike a "hegemonic bargain" in which they use one of several strategies to address the fact that they cannot meet the hegemonic ideal.[30] By using a hegemonic bargain, these men trade on the privileges that they have in other status categories to achieve some aspects of the hegemonic ideal. Using strategies like compensation, deflection, denial, or repudiation, these men are able to acquire status where they can "make up" for racial stigmatization, thereby achieving some aspects of hegemonic power and privilege.

Other studies of black men reveal ways they attempt to follow a similar process to achieve the status associated with hegemonic masculinity. In their study of working-class and working-poor black men in an urban area, Richard Majors and Janet Billson contend that black men adopt a "cool pose" as a strategy for achieving masculinity.[31] Given that these men face occupational and educational challenges that preclude using middle-class employment as a strategy for achieving hegemonic masculinity, embracing the cool pose—eschewing emotion and sentiment—allows them to construct a viable performance of masculinity. Like the men in Chen's study, they are able to highlight the available avenues for achieving masculinity despite the fact that racial stigma (and its connection to issues of class, education, and employment) means other routes are closed to them.[32]

Still other studies reveal ways that black men reject the hegemonic masculine ideal and instead construct a marginalized masculinity that prizes alternative characteristics and behaviors. In Michele Lamont's study of working-class black and white men in France and the United States, she finds that black men stress the importance of being concerned for the well-being of others as a critical component of masculinity.[33] These men develop what Lamont refers to as a "caring self," in which they highlight values like "morality, solidarity, and generosity."[34] Significantly, the caring self develops as a consequence of their own experiences with racism and injustice. As these men are subjected to racial inequality, they develop a marginalized masculinity that is defined in part by a willingness to fight on behalf of others.

My own research involving black male nurses also highlights a form of marginalized masculinity that differs from the hegemonic ideal.[35] In a profession dominated by white women, black male nurses encounter numerous cases of gendered racism at work. In response, they develop a marginalized masculinity that enables them to offset the feminization associated with their work environments. Therefore, when patients and colleagues suggest that black male nurses are not qualified or capable of performing well in their jobs, the nurses respond by emphasizing their ability to embrace caring as a true marker of masculinity and one that allows them to be highly competent nurses. Additionally, when they face gendered racism that constrains their ability to access higher-status jobs in the profession, black male nurses focus on the status that they have outside the profession and within the black community (unlike their white male peers, whose interest in higher-status jobs functions as a means of establishing masculinity). Thus, they construct a marginalized masculinity that is characterized by status outside of the workplace and comfort with, rather than rejection of, the display of emotion and empathy.

The current study indicates that black men in male-dominated occupations also construct marginalized masculinities. As with black men in the nursing profession, these masculinities allow them to counter the issues and problems they face in the workplace. These masculinities reflect the particular needs and social character of the occupation such that the men are much less likely to construct masculinities that emphasize empathy and emotional availability. Yet this is not to say these marginalized masculinities are solely about reaching the hegemonic ideal. Rather, black professional men construct paradigms of marginalized masculinity that reflect the workplace challenges they face while permitting a type of masculinity that allows them to succeed in environments where hegemonic masculinities are prized (but unavailable to them). I argue that black men develop one of three core marginalized masculinities in the workplace: the tough guy, the nonthreatening-at-all-costs guy, and the friendly-but-with-limits guy.

The Tough Guy

Several men in my sample shared that their masculine behavior at work takes the form of toughness, arrogance, combativeness, and, as one respondent succinctly put it, being "an asshole." In some male-dominated professions, forceful, hegemonic male behavior is expected or even rewarded.[36] The men in my sample describe engaging in assertive and domineering behavior not because it was consistent with the occupational culture of their jobs but as a way to offset the challenges they encountered at work.

Welton, the doctor, provides an example of how he reacts to nurses who treat him in a manner that he perceives as disrespectful:

> So you [a nurse] come and tell me how I *better* not do this and I *better* not do that, and we're out in the middle of the clinic? I

will tear you a new one and explain to you. I call them out on it! I go, "I don't know what your issue is, but if you're not going to go up and talk to that [white] doctor like that, don't you come up in my face and talk to me like that! You got something to say to me, then you take it where it's got to go, or you ask for the time to make an appointment to speak to me. Otherwise, don't talk to me." And they'll go—their feelings are hurt—and cry to another doctor, and that doctor [will say], "Oh, you can't be like that to an employee." And I'm like, "Wait a minute, when's the last time a nurse came up and told you that you better not do something or that you did this and you did that and don't do it again?" If she doesn't do it to you, don't do it to me. So for the subordinates, what I would do early on is I'd embarrass them. Just straight up. I don't care. (Emphasis in original.)

As Welton describes, he pulls no punches when it comes to correcting subordinates whom he perceives as disrespectfully challenging his authority. Notably, the primary issue that piques his ire is the more deferential manner in which he observes white female nurses treating white male doctors. Consequently, by displaying a no-nonsense, assertive masculinity, Welton seeks to gain the respect due him in the workplace.

To an extent, the issues that drive Welton to display the tough guy form of masculinity can be interpreted as an example of what happens when black male workers are treated in accordance with the informal "impostor" role. As Welton describes, the nurses in question do not treat him in the same fashion as they do white male doctors. Thus, in response to being cast as an impostor—someone who does not deserve the level of respect and esteem accorded white male doctors—Welton enacts the tough guy masculinity to correct this.

Brody, the partnered lawyer, also talks about adopting the tough guy stance at work. In his case, however, Brody uses the tough guy masculinity not in response to disrespectful treatment from subordinates but to aid other black lawyers in the firm:

Sometimes people who support you can be jerks, and people you're comfortable with will backstab you. People can be passive-aggressive—they'll stop working with people rather than giving them feedback; then they'll look at minority lawyers' hours and ask how we can justify keeping them on. That's because they can give candid feedback to whites but not blacks. My former mentor gave it to me straight. He told me my work was crap, but this helped me to do better. So I try to share that bluntness, but I do it to help. Because I know black lawyers are getting evaluated on this, even if people won't do it openly or give them the tools to help. I'll be the jerk, the asshole, but it's because it's what you need to improve. But also, this is the way the white guys treat other white associates. But they'll tiptoe around the black guys because they don't know how to talk to them.

Brody provides an interesting perspective on the tough guy role. For him, it helps counterbalance how he sees black associates being treated. Essentially, Brody argues he is imitating the method of delivering highly critical feedback that white partners use to help white associates improve. This is particularly necessary in the context of the firm because he observes that black lawyers are not getting this important feedback, and they are then criticized when their performance falls short. In this regard, then, being the "tough guy" simply approximates the type of masculinity white male partners exhibit when interacting with white male associates but fail to adopt when working with black lawyers.

In this case, Brody—unlike Welton, who adopts the tough guy model in reaction to his role as impostor—employs tough guy masculinity to help other black male lawyers confronted with the informal role of the superbrother. Given that many respondents talk about the expectation that they have to be prodigiously capable to be considered acceptable, any errors and mistakes on their part carry heightened significance. Thus, when Brody becomes a tough guy, it is a form of masculinity that helps address some of the adverse consequences black men encounter as a result of the superbrother role.

In some situations, tough guy masculinity yields negative results. Attorney Randy talks about the disadvantages of this type of masculinity:

Everyone knows me; I'm not going to take any shit. I'll take it once or twice, and I'm done with you, and so I'll say something to you. [I'm] just not the one to mess with. If you say something to [me] the wrong way or, you know, you're certainly not going to yell at [me] 'cause [I'm] going to yell back at you. [I'm] going to call you out, and if you're not happy with something, you need to present it to [me] in such a way that isn't aggressive 'cause [I'll] say something to you. [I'm] confrontational; [I'm] not afraid of the fight. [For example,] one partner here wanted something fast. He gave it to me to do, and I couldn't get to it for a while, so he took it from me. He gave it to someone else who took another two months to do it. He had a problem with me not doing it in a week and a half, but he let somebody else sit on something for a month and a half. I call that the old black tax. What the hell? I can have two weeks to do something, but you give this other individual two months to do it? But then you go behind my back and talk trash about me in the office. "You know, Randy didn't do such and such, so and so, in the allotted time I gave him." But you don't tell the other side of the story, which is I gave it to somebody else who took three times as long as the time I gave him. [I confronted him], so he knows not to talk to me in that way. You can give that vibe [of] don't even walk in my office with that.

I was very surprised that Randy would choose to speak and interact this way with a partner, and I shared my feelings with him during the interview. Extensive research suggests that ties to partners are extremely important for success in law firms, and my own data reveal that black male attorneys are particularly aware of the disadvantages of having weak or nonexistent relationships with partners; therefore, I was taken aback that Randy would be so openly confrontational. When I raised this point to him, he replied:

See, that's always been my problem. I don't see the difference, and I understand that partners deserve a certain level of respect. But you have to also understand, I'm just not going to cower down to you. If you're wrong, you're wrong. At big shops, big law firms, you kind of drop your head, and you get a lot of partners who get away with anything. But you have to remember, I'm also a little older. So they're only like forty-two, forty-four—and they're a partner—and I'm thirty-nine. So you're not that far off, buddy. So this talking down [to me]? No, uh-uh. You try that with a twenty-four-year-old, twenty-six-year-old, not me. But it has its drawbacks. 'Cause you don't want to deal with me now. I'm seen as obstinate. I'm seen as an aggressor, potentially. I'm seen as, "Oh no, I got to deal with his ass and his attitude." And granted, it hurts now, financially, sometimes, because you've got two people to go to. You've got the white cat, who you know is going to do it by the book, keep his head down, won't say anything, you may treat like crap. But then you got Randy over there and all of his complexities. I'm going to take my ass over here to this white cat.

Simply put, Randy is willing to accept the consequences—both financial and professional—of being "confrontational" and "not afraid of the fight." However, it is also worth noting that at the time of our interview, Randy had chosen to leave a large firm that he described as a poor fit for his style as a lawyer and his personality. He characterized his current place of employment as "less restrictive" than larger firms and where "everyone has their quirks."

The instances in which Randy describes being the tough guy were sparked in response to a partner's expectation that he complete a task in an unrealistic amount of time. Like the example Brody gives, Randy seems here to be held to the superbrother informal role. Rather than accept this position, he adopts the tough guy form of masculinity as a way to challenge a stereotyped informal role that does not fit.

The Nonthreatening-at-All-Costs Guy

Another type of marginalized masculinity in the workplace has men portraying themselves as nonthreatening. In this portrayal, men make it a point to depict themselves as easygoing, approachable, and placid. Their goal is that colleagues find them safe, comfortable, and relatively relatable. In particular, they work to make sure whites never find them menacing, challenging, or potentially dangerous.

In previous chapters, I discuss the specter of the "angry black man" and its influence on the dynamics of black professional men's workplace relationships and interactions. (I address this in more detail in the next chapter.) The marginalized masculinity embodied in the nonthreatening guy is a direct response to this broader controlling image. Black professional men are well aware that they are easily cast as angry black men, and they are also cognizant of how this cultural image informs some of the stereotyped roles they encounter in the workplace. The impostor role, in particular, tends to incorporate some aspects of this image, especially inasmuch as it relies on the characterization of black men as people who are dangerous and scary. By exhibiting the marginalized masculinity of the nonthreatening guy, some black men work to offset the counterimage of themselves as fearsome individuals.

Larry, the engineer in his twenties, talks about adopting this type of masculinity as a way to ensure his involvement in integral office networks:

> It's more strategy, you know. 'Cause no one really knows—none of them really knew me. They didn't really know much about me. They did know that I was highly educated for the position. I was overeducated for the position, because at that point I had two master's degrees, and I also had a Cisco certification, so I was better qualified than any of them to do whatever. So they knew that about me, and I was really witty. You know, they make little jokes or whatever, and my comebacks would be zingers. So I was funny. And I wasn't threatening. Even though I'm large in stature, physically, I'm less threatening because, when the time comes, I can speak a certain way and I can relate to a certain culture. So I guess, for them, I was less threatening.

For Larry, using humor was a strategy that enabled him to appear nonthreatening, despite a physical appearance that might have given the opposite impression. Larry is more than six feet tall and rather heavyset—he could conceivably be an intimidating presence to some. However, being the nonthreatening guy is a type of masculinity that helps ease interactions with his colleagues.

Later on in our interview, Larry expands on how he makes certain to avoid coming off as threatening. He compares a previous job to his current one, saying that, previously, he had to be a completely different person to be less threatening:

[Before], I wouldn't do the beard thing. I [didn't] speak loudly. Now I speak louder than I've ever spoken before. I was normally kind of a—the bass was kind of turned down in my voice. It sickens me to think about it. And just, generally, being more approachable—like I wouldn't put my headphones on at my desk. I'd try to keep my desk somewhat clean. 'Cause I'm a junky person. It gets me in a lot of trouble with my wife, but I don't have to—it doesn't have to be clean for me. So now [at my current job,] my desk is a wreck. Someone said, "Let me borrow your scissors." I'm like, "If you can find them, you can use them." Where before, the desk was really clean. And all this stuff wasn't there. Like now I do pictures. You know, I'm probably the only person with pictures. But because in my previous role, everyone had pictures of their kids, their wife, and they're in their Sunday best. It's all a nice little charade. And I did that.

The contrast between Larry's previous job (in a work environment he did not particularly enjoy and he felt stifled him) and his current one highlights the toll nonthreatening masculinity can take on black male workers. Note that adopting this role is not particularly pleasant for Larry; he characterizes it as "a charade" and says that it "sickens him" to think about his portraying this kind of masculinity in the workplace. However, Larry describes this role as a way of fitting in with colleagues who otherwise may exclude him from important social networks. Though he does not go into extensive detail about these processes, it is possible that Larry's exclusion may be a consequence of being viewed through the stereotyped informal role of the impostor, wherein coworkers fail to view him as someone who truly belongs in the social networks that allow for advancement.

Lionel, the emergency room doctor, also talks about employing this nonthreatening masculinity:

You know, the world to me does not tolerate the angry, irate black male. So I'm rarely, rarely that. I *can* be and have moments when I've done it, but if that's your regular operating principle and pattern, you will not survive here. And it's interesting, because we have somebody who—a recent VP who came here—that I won't say was angry but certainly had the irritable black male behavior pattern, and it was instantaneously bothersome to the people that worked here across pretty much every level, actually. So certainly, the white males did not tolerate him very well. White females didn't. But even some black males, you know, didn't tolerate it well themselves. The world doesn't tolerate black men—irritable, angry black men. They just don't. (Emphasis in original.)

Because of Lionel's perceptions of how the angry black man is received, he makes certain that he comes across as nonthreatening and affable—a stark contrast to this image.

Rodney, the former banking executive, also talks about the need to come across as nonthreatening:

I have a very deep voice, I'm six foot two, I'm a darker-skinned man. . . . Is that something that is sort of off-putting [to] some people? I don't know. I wonder sometimes if maybe the fact that—do I have to [make changes]? So I started lowering my [voice], maybe to see if that would give them a different impression—so that I wouldn't be as threatening to them.

As Rodney describes, his physical appearance can potentially be threatening to others who subscribe to the stereotypes about black men being dangerous and menacing. Consequently, he attempts to adjust his voice and behavior to offset this.

In each of these cases, men acknowledge that black men are generally perceived as people who pose a threat. This may inform how they are subjected to the stereotyped informal role of the impostor. If black men are viewed as people who are generally dangerous, they may be less likely to be seen as people who fit the cultural concept of doctors, lawyers, bankers, or engineers. Given that this threatening image is a widespread, longstanding one in the cultural imagination, black professional men adopt the marginalized masculinity of the nonthreatening guy as a way to respond to and challenge this representation.

The Friendly-but-with-Limits Guy

A third type of marginalized masculinity that the men in my study enact is the guy who is friendly and cordial but could be assertive if need be. I refer to this as the friendly-but-with-limits guy. With this type of masculinity, respondents present themselves as men who are affable, genial types. However, they also take care to depict themselves as men whose niceness should not be taken advantage of by others. In short, they are sociable and pleasant, but if pushed or mistreated, they can morph into tough guys who do not accept disrespectful treatment.

By constructing this type of masculinity, black men are able to walk a line between the previously described forms of masculinity. They can enjoy the benefits of being men who are nice, affable, and pleasant, but at the same time, they adopt aspects of tough guy masculinity that protect them when they are confronted with stereotyped informal roles that lead to negative treatment. Jason, the corporate lawyer, provides a general description of how he can morph from friendly to tough: "I can turn on 'aggressive black man in bear mode' if I need to. But it's rare that I need to, and it does—it can do so much harm. You let people know that it's there, and it communicates a strong message, and you do it in a measured way." As Jason says, he can become the tough guy who makes it clear that limits of acceptability have been breached. However, he also acknowledges that this is a strategy to be used rarely, as it can have negative consequences itself.

In another example, Larry, the engineer, describes the way that his friendly-but-with-limits masculinity contrasts with that of his white boss, who faces less pressure to corral the tougher side of his persona:

> I hear him giving someone the business really loud and really, really aggressive. And just really being an asshole. Now when I, in a situation where it becomes necessary for me to speak up and to make a strong stance, you know, he tells me that I'm being— he's always like, "Calm down. There's a different way of saying that." Or "Don't be so—don't take it so personally." And some of it is I've grown tired of masking myself, really. For me, I'm on my exit strategy. I'm not doing my vertical strategy; I'm on my exit strategy. So my tolerance to keep up the charade is very

low. So he's seeing more of who I am than anyone else is seeing. So a lot of times, there's things I'm going to call, and I'm trying to express myself, and if there's someone there who for whatever reason is just not getting it—or either they get it, but they just don't want to hear it—then I may become more aggressive than I normally am. But it's hundreds of times less aggressive than . . . how he is on a call. Because he's commonly thought of as an asshole. But he can do that, and I can't. I'm not a big yeller, but if I think something is not right, then I'm going to say, I mean, "You can't do that. What you're saying doesn't make sense." And I make a hard stance, or I might make a definitive statement, but I'm not yelling or huffing or puffing and all this stuff.

Several important themes emerge in Larry's statement. First, he highlights the contrast between the way he is sometimes challenged when he becomes tough and the way his boss is able to be "the asshole" with few repercussions, suggesting that as a black male, the ability to be too straightforward is often constrained. Second, he gives some insights into the parameters of this particular type of masculinity. Specifically, Larry's friendly-but-tough persona extends to being more honest and direct when he perceives that someone is making a mistake or an error. In contrast to his boss, he does not believe that he can acceptably become aggressive, shout, or "huff and puff" to get his points across. Thus, this type of masculinity involves being assertive rather than confrontational.

Mitch, the emergency room doctor, talks about establishing this friendly-but-tough masculinity in very clear terms:

Being a successful black man, being assertive is not something that comes new. You have to be that in order to get where you are. If you've gotten to this point, you figure out how to be assertive and not come across as the angry black man or so forth. I know a lot of physicians will deal with [some situations] very passive-aggressive. They'll yell at people on the phone, and then the person on the other line will just sit there and hang up the phone and then talk bad about the person. Whereas I know that's just not me. I will say, "Look, don't talk to me like that. This is what needs to be done; either you're going to do it, or I'll

call someone else and get them paid for it; it's not a big deal."
And, you know, you don't make friends that way; there's no
question about it. But you don't have to deal with it after that—
after the first couple of times.

For Mitch, establishing a masculinity that shows that he has his limits and is not someone to be treated poorly allows him to assert himself
as someone to be respected, while avoiding the image of the angry
black man.

Ultimately, these men create and embody a third type of masculinity wherein they are generally welcoming, friendly people who make it
clear that their kindness is not to be abused or exploited. This allows
black men to avoid the negative stereotypes that accompany the angry
black man image but still permits them to toughen up when necessary
in response to deleterious or poor treatment. Friendly-but-with-limits
masculinity lets these men navigate the pitfalls associated with both the
tough guy and the nonthreatening masculine personas.

Summary

This chapter assesses partial tokenization in terms of its impact on the
stereotyped informal roles black men face and the masculinities they
construct as a consequence. As Kanter writes, those in the numerical minority are subject to stereotyped informal roles that intensify
the challenges they face assimilating into the majority.[37] However, the
roles she describes—the pet, the iron maiden, the seductress, and the
mother—are clearly gender (and probably racially) specific. As such,
they are inapplicable to black men who work in predominantly white,
masculine settings.

As I have demonstrated, though, this by no means indicates that
black men are exempt from stereotyped informal roles. Instead, they
encounter roles that are shaped by intersections of race and gender,
and these roles are likely unique to them because of the particular stereotypes associated with black masculinity. Black men thus cope with
being cast as the impostor, the superbrother, and/or the race representative—roles that, like the ones ascribed to the women in Kanter's
study, are confining and impede their ability to fully assimilate into the

dominant group.[38] After all, if black men are perceived as impostors, this clearly creates additional barriers to their fitting seamlessly into the work environment. When black men are treated as superbrothers, the unreasonably high expectations associated with this role make their realistic accomplishments seem dull by comparison and, more important, make them seem less exceptional relative to their white male counterparts. Finally, if black men are cast as race representatives, this highlights the ways in which they stand out from members of the dominant group and can create additional work that prevents them from meeting their defined job duties.

One of the strategies available to black men when faced with these stereotyped informal roles involves the development and enactment of various forms of masculinity. Here, intersections of race and gender are paramount as well. Given the specter of the "angry black man" and the prevalence of this image in the cultural imagination, black men must be careful about how they construct masculine performances in the workplace. They are not necessarily permitted to enact the same types of masculinity attributed to white men in the workplace, because performances that require aggressiveness, dominance, or forceful behavior may be viewed as threatening and intimidating coming from black men.[39] Thus, marginalized masculinities of the tough guy, the non-threatening-at-all-costs guy, or the friendly-but-with-limits guy offer reasonable alternatives that allow black men to respond to the stereotyped informal roles they encounter while still navigating the precarious terrain of avoiding the angry black man image.

The findings in this chapter have important implications for what sociologists know about processes of tokenization, performances of masculinity, and the specifically racialized and gendered challenges black professional men address. Black men's experiences with stereotyped informal roles echo Kanter's early argument that those in the numerical minority do indeed face these depictions, but the particular ways they are constructed for black men suggest that these informal roles are hardly generalizable or consistent across all groups.[40] Rather, assumptions about race and gender shape how stereotyped informal roles are constructed such that the white women in Kanter's study encounter roles that reflect assumptions about gender, race, and femininity, while black men in this study confront roles specifically shaped by the ways gender, race, and masculinity are differently embodied for men of color.[41]

Additionally, some existing studies analyze how men who are outside of the hegemonic masculine ideal construct marginalized masculinities.[42] This research builds on those studies by highlighting the numerical minority's connection to the performance of masculinity. More specifically, the partial tokenization of black men in white male–dominated jobs informs the stereotyped informal roles they face and the ways in which they develop marginalized masculinities that run counter to these roles. Masculinities, then, are not just connected to the organizational culture of a workplace and the context in which they are performed, but they reflect numerical standing and the complicated intersections of race and gender in the workplace.[43]

These findings about the performance of masculinity also have implications for studies of black professional workers. Research in this vein often lumps black male and black female professionals together, describing the challenges they face as gender-neutral or evenly applicable to both groups.[44] The studies that focus explicitly on black female professionals demonstrate that the problems they face—being hypersexualized and described as mean and cold—are a consequence of gendered and racial interactions that create specific, unique outcomes.[45] Yet black men's construction of marginalized masculinities suggests that they, like black women, encounter challenges in the professional workplace that also uniquely reflect the intersections of gender and race. Black men are not hypersexualized or seen as mean and cold in these masculine work environments, but they are subjected to stereotyped informal roles that complicate their ability to fit in completely with their white male colleagues.

6 | Emotional Performance

In previous chapters, I allude to the specter of the angry black man. When referring to this image, black male respondents are typically indicating a stereotype of black men as angry, vicious, and out of control. These representations of black masculinity offer a particular characterization of black men as needlessly volatile and potentially dangerous, inasmuch as their anger is cast as frequent, threatening, and unpredictable. As discussed, the image of the angry black man serves to temper black professional men's performances of masculinity and can inform how they interact with women in the workplace as well.

In this chapter, I build on this idea of the angry black man as a way of exploring black men's emotional performance in predominantly white male occupations. Given that the angry black man characterization is so encompassing for these men, it provides a critical framework for assessing how they construct emotional selves in these work environments. Thus, I turn here to partial tokenization and its influence on black men's emotional performance.

Black Professionals' Anger

Outside of the discipline of sociology, journalist Ellis Cose has devoted a great deal of attention to tracking and documenting the emotional toll that can accompany being black in the professional workplace. In his aptly titled study *The Rage of a Privileged Class*, Cose asserts that black workers in high status, professional positions are experiencing an emotional struggle that goes largely overlooked and unrecognized.[1] Based on interviews with friends, colleagues, and other contacts, Cose contends that members of the black elite have mixed feelings about their occupational successes: they feel proud and humbled by their accomplishments and successes; however, this pride is often mixed with a sense of futility, bitterness, and sometimes rage as they reflect on the heights they would have been able to reach had racial barriers not stood in their way. Cose begins *The Rage of a Privileged Class* in this way:

> Despite its very evident prosperity, much of America's black middle class is in excruciating pain. And that distress—although most of the country does not see it—illuminates a serious American problem: the problem of the broken covenant, of the pact ensuring that if you work hard, get a good education, and play by the rules, you will be allowed to advance and achieve to the limits of your ability.[2]

Cose notes that these members of the black elite, who seem to have everything, often simmer with rage as they become aware that despite their hard work, efforts, and willingness to "play by the rules," race still remains an insurmountable obstacle that prevents them from reaching their full potential.[3]

What stands out from Cose's interviews and accounts in this book are the feelings of anger, frustration, and bitterness articulated by many of his respondents. Having bought into the notion that hard work and effort would be rewarded, quite a few of the black professionals with whom Cose speaks are very upset that this ideology has not proven to be true for them. This study therefore tackles an important aspect of life for black professional workers by considering the emotional toll racial discrimination and inequality take on them, particularly when they have ascended to positions that offer high status and great economic reward.

Recently, Cose revisited this theme of exploring the emotional state of black professional workers. However, his results this time are markedly different.[4] Cose argues that the simmering rage he uncovered in 1993 has generally evaporated. Instead, he finds that members of younger generations are more likely to approach the future with equanimity and optimism. While they are under no illusions that racism has been completely eradicated, they "[see] a world in which race seriously affects opportunities for blacks and Hispanics, but (and this is a crucial 'but') not strongly enough to prevent them from getting where they want to go."[5] Titling this book *The End of Anger*, Cose paints an optimistic portrait of a younger generation of blacks and whites who have largely eschewed the anger of their predecessors as they become poised to enter a work world that they perceive to be more fair, equitable, and accepting.[6]

Cose's work offers a useful, if general assessment of the emotional state of black professionals.[7] His discussion of the transition from anger to hopefulness gives a sense of the broad challenges facing black professional workers as well as some of the structural and social changes that inform younger blacks' emotional demeanor. Yet there are likely additional factors that shape the emotional expressions of black professionals, particularly black professional men in white male–dominated occupations. Sociological theories can help shed light on this.

Tokens' Emotions

In her work, Rosabeth Moss Kanter only touches on the emotional responses that are likely to ensue from the process of tokenization.[8] In particular, she considers the impact that the pressures of heightened visibility, contrast, and assimilation have on those in the numerical minority and concludes that the emotional toll these processes take on the token is intense. Kanter writes:

> Even the best coping strategy is likely to have some internal repercussions, ranging from *inhibition of self-expression to feelings of inadequacy and, perhaps, self-hatred* . . . to the extent that tokens accept their exceptional status, dissociate themselves from others of their category, and turn against them, tokens may be denying parts of themselves and engaging in self-hatred. This can produce inner tension. (Emphasis added.)[9]

Kanter thus theorizes that tokenization has an emotional component—it leads those in the minority to experience emotions of inadequacy and self-hatred and likely induces feelings of stress and tension.

Other than these short points, Kanter does not devote much more analytical space to addressing the ways that tokenization can influence emotional performance among those in the minority.[10] However, her claims leave much more room for analysis of how being in the minority can affect emotions. For addressing this issue in more detail, the research on sociology of emotions is perhaps more instructive.

Arlie Hochschild's framework of emotional labor has proven ground-breaking in assessing some of the dynamics of emotions in various settings, but particularly in the workplace.[11] In her seminal work *The Managed Heart*, Hochschild argues that the rise of the service economy has created a commercialization of feeling.[12] Specifically, service jobs do not require workers to create products, but they are expected to manifest and express emotions and instill them in others. One of the consequences of this is that employees' emotions are subjected to organizational oversight to the point where workers may feel that management actually owns and controls their very feelings. Thus, employees may find themselves creating emotions that they do not necessarily feel in exchange for wages.

One of the most significant parts of Hochschild's analysis involves the gendered patterns that emerge among workers.[13] Studying flight attendants and bill collectors, she argues that the emotions that organizations mandate from employees differ depending on the gendered composition of jobs. Flight attendants—who are mostly women—are expected to make passengers feel secure, comforted, and safe; in contrast, mostly male bill collectors make debtors feel intimidated and afraid. The emotions that these workers are expected to instill are consistent with gendered ideas about masculinity and femininity. Thus, organizations establish institutional mandates wherein men and women employees reproduce gendered behaviors.

An additional aspect of Hochschild's research involves the distinctions between various types of emotional performance.[14] Specifically, she differentiates emotional labor, emotion management/emotion work, and feeling rules. *Emotional labor* occurs when emotions are produced in oneself or in others in exchange for a wage—in other words, when emotions take on exchange value. This involves the sort of emotional exchange I describe above—flight attendants and bill collectors evoking emotions in themselves as part of their jobs. Other studies have added to this by documenting emotional labor among insurance and fast food workers, attorneys, paralegals and legal secretaries, nursing home workers, and numerous other occupational roles.[15]

Yet Hochschild is also clear about the boundaries between emotional labor and other sorts of emotional performance.[16] She regards *emotion work*, or *emotion management* (terms she uses interchangeably), as how people adjust their feelings to fit emotional norms in everyday contexts. Thus, people who display happiness for a friend or feel sympathy for a colleague might engage in emotion management. These people are not altering their emotions for wages but shifting their affect in the many everyday social situations in which we are expected to display the appropriate emotional demeanor for the given context.

Finally, Hochschild contends that feeling rules serve to establish and define the "correct" emotional norms that are present in a given situation.[17] As such, if a friend tells me that she is getting married, the *feeling rules* of that situation might dictate that I should feel happy for her. If I dislike her fiancé, however, I might need to do emotion management and conceal my distaste while allowing my feelings of happiness and support to shine through. These feeling rules lay the groundwork for emotion management that is done in everyday settings, as well as for the emotional labor that occurs in occupational arenas.

By defining these core terms, Hochschild's work provides a useful theoretical paradigm for exploring various aspects of emotional performance in a wide array of settings.[18] In particular, these sociological concepts serve to conceptualize emotional performance within the workplace, where organizational norms, rules, and regulations have particular significance for employees' demeanor, feelings, and self-presentation. Yet one of the omissions of Hochschild's original study is that it does not give much attention to how the racial dynamics that shape occupational processes and the work experience, more generally, inform emotional performance.[19] In the next section, I turn to the more recent research that examines the ways race can affect workers' emotional performance.

Race and Emotion Management

Though the sociology of emotions literature has generated a wealth of influential data about how emotional performance reproduces gendered hierarchies, researchers in this area have not been as adept at considering emotion management and race. As Kiran Mirchandani observes, this is a major shortcoming in the extant research and one that leads to a host of unanswered questions about emotion management.[20] For instance, the existing research documents that women are expected to perform more traditionally "feminine" emotions, such as caretaking, deference, and nurturing, particularly in occupations where they interact with higher-status males.[21] Women who fail to perform this emotional labor run the risk of being typed as shrill, unfeminine, or less competent at their jobs. However, given that women of color often face racialized, gendered stereotypes that paint them as mean, aggressive, and/or domineering, it is worth considering whether they face particular challenges conforming to the emotional demands expected in their jobs. For instance, given the stereotype of Asian American women as dragon ladies, does it become more difficult for them to meet the emotional norms of deference and caretaking that are required for women who work as paralegals or flight attendants?[22] Conversely, does the opposing image of Asian American women as lotus blossoms create heightened expectations of docility and passivity that are mapped onto their work in these arenas?[23]

As of late, some studies have begun to investigate related questions to consider the ways that race influences emotional performance in various jobs. Miliann Kang's analysis of Korean immigrant women nail technicians is one such example.[24] In her ethnographic study of these women, Kang argues that existing paradigms of emotional labor fail to take into consideration the upsurge in work that involves both emotional management and work on the body.[25] Thus, she introduces the term *body labor* to encapsulate both the physical and emotional labor that is a critical part of certain jobs.

Building on this, Kang contends that race, gender, and class intersect to shape the emotional labor that goes into Korean manicurists' work.[26] Depending on the clientele these women are servicing, certain forms of emotional labor become more prevalent and useful. When working with upper-class white women, nail technicians are more likely to invoke a pampering labor that meets customers' expectations and desires. In contrast, service interactions with working-class black women customers requires expressive labor that recognizes and displays appreciation, particularly given the sometimes fraught relationship that exists between black and Korean communities. Finally, manicurists who work in one-size-fits-all, quickie shops do a routinized labor that meets their multiracial customer base's need for efficient, speedy service.

Kang's research here fills important gaps in the emotion work literature.[27] This research demonstrates that the race, gender, and class of both the worker and the customer in this service interaction inform the emotional labor that is performed. Additionally, broader racial histories and imagery (of Asian American women as particularly subservient and suited for service work, of tensions between black and Korean communities) have implications for how workers determine what sort of emotional labor is most appropriate in particular occupational contexts.

Roxana Harlow's study of black college and university professors helps add further dimensions to the research on emotional performance.[28] She argues that racial stigma affects the ways these faculty members are perceived and evaluated by white students. Black professors in this study find that white students often see them as less qualified, less capable, and less well trained than their white counterparts. These professors respond by doing emotion work to conceal their feelings of irritation and annoyance, instead emphasizing feelings of professionalism and competency. Black women professors, in particular, encounter gendered and racialized characterizations that cast them as "mean" and "cold," and thus they do emotion work that rebuts these specific depictions. Harlow's work echoes Kang's research about the significance of race, but their conclusions also show that this sort of emotional performance may occur even when it is not given exchange value and explicitly requested by management.[29]

My research on black professionals and emotion work also emphasizes the role race plays in this arena. My recent study of black workers in professional occupations reveals that race shapes the feeling rules that guide their emotional performance in the workplace.[30] Black professionals contend that rather than being premised on neutral, objective criteria, feeling rules are instead based on racialized norms that do not necessarily extend to them. Using Kanter's theory of tokenism here as well, I argue that this process places black workers in a position in which they are less likely to be able to conform to certain feeling rules because of the racialized dynamics they encounter both within and outside of the workplace and that there are rules that are off-limits to them as members of the numerical minority.[31]

In a finding that has key relevance for this study, I contend that the emotion of anger is particularly salient for black professionals and reflects intersections of race and gender. In my research, black professional workers argue that one of the critical areas where they are held to different feeling rules than their white counterparts involves the emotion of anger. Respondents observe that the feeling rules of their work environments legitimize expressions of anger from white colleagues. However, black workers do not feel that they are permitted to show this emotion, particularly if it arises in response to racial issues.

Significantly, black men feel pressured to conceal feelings of frustration, irritation, and annoyance, particularly compared to their black female counterparts. Note this remark from a black male systems engineer:

> One woman—management had a problem with her, with one of her presentations. The organization [of her presentation] wasn't tight, and she went off! "What is it now? You guys are really getting on my nerves!" And I'm like, "Wow, she's talking to managers like that?" She's still there; nothing's wrong. They met with her—I heard her threaten to quit—and they were like, "No, don't quit!" If it were me, they'd probably be like, "All right!" You know? So they [whites] say what they want. If someone says, "Do this," they question it, or they get smart. If it was me, I'd be labeled as an angry black dude—can't get along with coworkers. But because it's them, it's all right.[32]

Here, this respondent indicates the way that the stereotype of the angry black man, along with his observations about organizational expectations, helps shape his perception that unlike white colleagues, he is not permitted to show anger. In contrast, consider this black female respondent's viewpoint:

The main thing I had to control was not snapping on people. Why do I have to be in educator mode all the time and always have to explain how stupid what you just said was? So the main feelings I had to control were feelings of irritation and frustration. There was just no way to come in to work as angry as I sometimes was. But you know what? I took full advantage of the fact that they were a little afraid of me. Sometimes it gave me the space to say what I needed to say. It was frustrating that they didn't want to get better at relating to people who were different. So I said, "This is what I'm feeling," and came right out with it. I did not always need to manage my emotions.[33]

Unlike the male respondent, this female community educator argues that using anger strategically can be a way of being taken more seriously. This was not a response that is universally expressed among the women in my sample, but it does surface often enough to suggest gender disparities between black men and women in terms of how, and the extent to which, black respondents feel they can follow the feeling rule of showing anger and frustration.

This 2010 study builds on the existing literature that asserts black professionals are likely to be tokenized in predominantly white workplaces through processes of exclusion, marginalization, and social isolation.[34] Yet this research also offers an empirical basis for asserting that the experience of tokenism affects not only black workers' occupational lives but also important aspects of their emotion work. Consequently, "black professionals are scrutinized not only for what they *do*, but what they *feel*" (emphasis in original).[35] Thus, as black professionals tend to be in the numerical minority in their occupations and encounter processes of tokenization, this extends to shape the emotions they are expected to reveal and conceal in predominantly white workplaces.

Each of these studies indicates that race matters in shaping the ways workers of color engage in emotional performance. Kang's work demonstrates that intersections of race, gender, and class matter for employees engaged in service work, while Harlow's research points to the emotion management black workers do that is not mandated by the workplace but that helps them cope with the consequences of racial stereotypes and misperceptions.[36] Finally, my own research on black professionals provides perhaps the closest theoretical and empirical leverage for this study by highlighting the particular emotion work of black men and how the derogatory social and cultural images attributed to them can inform their emotional performance in the workplace.

My previous work on black men reveals that the angry black man image influences these males' emotion management. In the remainder of this chapter, I build on previous studies of race and emotion management (including my own) to consider how the experience of partial tokenization affects black professional men's emotion work in male-dominated jobs.

Partial Tokenization and Emotion Work

For most of my respondents, discussions around emotions surface in only two arenas. Black professional men generally talk about having to control their emotions when it comes to expressions of anger and the need to present an unemotional demeanor in other contexts. Surprisingly, however, black professional men in this study are less focused on concealing all expressions of anger. In fact, they note becoming angry in certain cases, which is a contrast to my earlier research documenting their unwillingness to display this emotion. Paradoxically, though, many respondents also discuss the need to maintain an unemotional, detached demeanor.

Getting Angry in Spite of the Angry Black Man

There were a few respondents who, consistent with previous studies, talk about their perception that they simply cannot afford to show anger in the workplace. Jason, the lawyer, talks about this in the context of how colleagues expect black men to approach them:

> What they expect is for us to come, sort of, with some level of anger that is identifiable. Some of us do, unfortunately. They expect us first to come to them as victims. And some of us do, unfortunately. They expect for us to come with some level of cynicism and distrust—not unearned, but they expect us to come with some arm's-length cynicism and distrust, and a lot

of us don't disappoint. And it's not to say that I'm myopic or pie-in-the-sky or, you know, in denial about what the deal is, but what I am saying is that I have found it to be a better strategy to give people what they don't expect.

As Jason describes, his perception is that white colleagues expect black men to have an angry, confrontational demeanor. By doing the emotion work of refusing to show anger, Jason circumvents these expectations.

Yet Jason's answer in this context is not necessarily representative. In conducting this research, I am particularly struck by the comments of other respondents who give themselves the freedom to get angry in response to injustices they experience in the workplace. Shawn, an engineer, talks about his perception that racial discrimination and cronyism on the part of white male supervisors kept him from getting a deserved promotion:

Even though I had never seen it [workplace discrimination] firsthand, per se, I mean, I knew things could be like that, you know. So I wasn't . . . shocked by it or anything. And I wasn't the first person [or] the last person who will deal with something like that. So I'm not going to say it was something I expected, but it was certainly something that I was aware that could happen. Was I a little bit angry? Yeah, *I was a little bit angry* 'cause I knew I had been cheated—you know what I mean. And I was seeing people getting privileges that I wasn't getting per se, even though they didn't deserve to get it any more than I did. So yeah, *that kind of pissed me off a little bit, and I won't say that I wasn't angry*, but, I mean, did I go home at night and cry about it? Nah. (Emphasis added.)

Here, Shawn does acknowledge that the discrimination he perceived at work did make him angry. He characterizes this by saying that he "was a little angry" about the way that he feels he was treated. Yet even this mild expression of anger represents a departure from previous research that suggests black men go out of their way to conceal this emotion.

In another case, Terrance, the engineer, talks about the perception of the angry black man and the impact it has on his self-presentation at work. He discusses this in the context of another black male employee who did come off in this fashion and the way in which this employee had to change to maintain his position in the organization:

> I think sometimes [that image] does [affect self-presentation at work]. I mean, [I'm] not saying I like to go along to get along, but, you know. I'll say things just to be combative sometimes, just to see what it would do, but that's just not my nature in general anyway, so I don't really come off like that. But I do get angry, and I do get frustrated that certain things aren't getting done, and I question that, but, you know, I think that's just not my nature, though. But some people are more aggressive, and I see that, and that perception can be out there. But like I said, [my job is] so virtual; it's just hard to see that sometimes. But I think [the other black male employee] came off like that when he first joined the company, but I think he even tempered it. He kind of had to.

Here, Terrance describes being intentionally combative in some cases, particularly when his group does not work together effectively. His statements suggest that while the angry black man image is something he is cognizant of, it does not necessarily lead him to feel that expressions of anger are prohibited at all costs.

The reactions from Terrance, Jason, and Shawn indicate that while the angry black man image is present and a factor in emotional performance, it is not a complete deterrent to the expression of this feeling. Black professional men may do some emotion management by concealing feelings of strong anger, annoyance, and irritation, but their experiences in male-dominated occupations do not place them in a position in which this emotion is something to be controlled in all circumstances.

As I argue in previous chapters, partial tokenization provides a more accurate way of assessing these men's emotional performance. While Kanter argues that tokenism leads those in the minority to experience emotional consequences of stress and self-hatred, other studies suggest that broader racial imagery can also affect emotion work.[37] Here, however, I find that being partially tokenized leaves black professional men able to show anger in some contexts, even if it is tempered and carefully expressed in light of the angry black man image.

Staying Unemotional

Respondents also discussed emotional performance in terms of maintaining a detached, uninflected demeanor. In many cases, these respondents did the emotion work of concealing a range of affect so as to appear largely impassive. Often, the men suppressed "negative" emotions, like annoyance, pain, or irritation. Thus, it should not be construed that Terrance's and Shawn's willingness to get angry is representative of black men's general experience. Rather, despite having the latitude to show anger in some situations, black professional men also do the emotion work of concealing emotions in response to certain issues, particularly those that relate to racial matters.

Richard, the emergency room doctor, offers one example of this. He describes repeated incidents that he attributes to the racial biases black men encounter in the medical field. He told me about two cases in which he experienced patients who doubted his capabilities and treated him suspiciously. I present both of Richard's descriptions to give the full context of his emotional response:

> I've had one experience where one person absolutely—no, two experiences—where someone absolutely refused to be treated. This person was actually dying and needed acute intervention to keep them from dying. And I walked in the room, and they expected me to—he was in severe respiratory distress and needed to be put on the ventilator relatively quickly. And he's gasping for air but saying, "I don't want you." I made sure he [understood he would die]. "I don't want you." His wife was sitting there. I said, "Okay," and I walked out. He was a grown man.

The second case Richard describes is remarkably similar:

> I'm the chairman of the emergency department where I work, and this guy was like, "I don't want you," and blah, blah, blah. And "I'm not going to be admitted by that Indian doctor either.

You guys need to get the hell out of here, and I want to talk to your supervisor! Who's the head of this department? Let me talk to him." And I turned around, and I said, "Oh wait, that's me." [He answered,] "Well that's bullshit. I don't believe you," you know. So I was like, dude [*pausing*]. So I just had security escort him out. I don't tolerate intolerance. I have very little tolerance for stupidity.

As Richard recounted these stories, I was struck by his dry, factual tone. He seemed disgusted but also very dismissive about incidents that he clearly considered to be motivated by outright racism. When I asked him about this response, he stated:

I don't have time for that. Those things don't bother me. It's like, whatever, you know. I'm black. I'm a doctor. . . . If you just want to be dumb, then be dumb. If you're going to be an idiot—you're going to sit here and die because you don't want a black person to put a tube in you—fine, die. You don't owe me. So [in the first case,] I walk out, and his wife runs down the hall; she's begging and pleading and holding on to my coat, and I'm like, just get off. It's clear that he didn't want me, so he'll have to get the Indian, the other, Indian doctor who's working today. Whatever. It happens. You don't want me to take care of you? Fine, then die. I'm going to walk out and have a sandwich. I have very little tolerance for that kind of stuff, so it's like I'm above caring.

As Richard says, he makes it a point not to allow patients' perceptions of his skills and capabilities make him angry or even emotionally invested. Thus, when confronted with occupational challenges that he perceives to be motivated by racism, Richard responds by doing the emotion work of expressing disinterest and showing an unemotional countenance.

Other respondents spoke more generally about the need to remain indifferent to stressors that could arise at work. Nathan, another of the emergency room doctors, offers an account that is similar to Richard's in terms of refusing to react to patients who reject treatment:

It's not offensive to me. In this particular instance, it's someone who has a real complaint, has a real disease—it doesn't make a difference, but you're uninsured, and I'm [still] willing to take care of you. And I'm happy to take care of you, and I'll take care of you just like you were my mom, brother, sister, neighbor. You don't want me to take care of you? You're a grown person. You're willing and able to make your own decisions; that's fine. It's my job to take care of people who want to be helped, not to take care of—I can't take care of everybody. So some people don't want to be helped, and some people have their own priorities and their own agenda, and that's fine. I didn't take offense to it. That's one less thing that I have to worry about for this time, and I can move on and take care of another person who's sick and is appreciative of [my] help. . . . And, obviously, if you can come to the hospital and make those types of decisions, then you're not that sick.

Like Richard, Nathan's emotion management consists of presenting an unruffled demeanor in response to issues that he sees as racially motivated. While he also attributes patients' refusal to let him treat them as a case of racial bias, he reacts to this by being detached and unaffected.

Mitch, another of the emergency room doctors, shares a story that is nearly identical to Richard's and Nathan's accounts:

I've been called "nigger" by my patients before and things like that. I tell them all the time—it doesn't matter who you are; I take care of you. It doesn't matter whether you're a murderer, a rapist, a racist. It doesn't matter in my job. My job is not to judge you; my job is to take care of you. But I've taken care of patients with swastikas and rebel flag ties and KKK tattoos and things like that all over them, and they made it very clear: "I'll sue you if you don't get me a white doctor." And it's funny because usually at night there's one of us there for three hours. There's a three-hour span where there's only one physician, so a lot of time I'll be like, "You can have a white doctor if you want to wait three hours to get seen by somebody," and I've had patients say, "That's fine. I'll go back out in the waiting room and wait until they come in at seven in the morning." *It doesn't bother me any*. I had a patient—I don't know what was going on with him, but he used the word *nigger* probably twelve times in a two-minute conversation, and I told him I didn't want to hear it any more; it upset other patients and other staff members around. *You know, I don't give a shit; go find a white doctor*. But, you know, that's not going to happen, and if you want to stay here, you're going to have to stop using that word, or I'll have to throw you out of the hospital. And I did; I ended up having to have him taken out. (Emphasis added.)

Again, what is illustrative about Mitch's narrative is the way in which he professes indifference to and a lack of concern over racial issues. Despite facing overt racial slurs from patients, Mitch describes his emotional reaction as detached and unaffected. His response shows another case of a black professional man doing the emotion work to present feelings of unflappability and impassiveness in response to racism.

Larry, the engineer, also talks at length in his interview about feeling his paths to upward mobility are more difficult to access relative to his white male counterparts. Yet he also expresses indifference as a means of dealing with this:

There's no growth for me here in this role. So I don't let it bother me. Like I tell my wife, it pays the bills. Now for someone like her—now she would be more—it would just kill her to not feel good about what you do. I'm indifferent. I have the ability to just tune stuff out, so I'm just tuning out. I guess maybe the disdain I feel for the role is tuned out. So I say, as long as no one is honing me in or yelling at me or trying to cut my face, then I can deal with it.

As Larry notes, tuning out his disdain for some aspects of his work environment helps him to cope with the frustration and annoyance he feels at times. Thus, like Richard, Nathan, and Mitch, he exhibits the emotion work of disinterest and indifference.

Richard talks in more detail about this process of developing the hard edge that enables him to show the emotions of unconcern in these situations:

> [Whites] are going to take care of themselves first and foremost, and they will step on other people. And as long as you understand the rules of the game, you can play. If you don't understand the rules of the game, you can't play. It just starts to get salty and "why this" and "why me," and this just—sort of what I call the loser mentality. [The main rule is] no trust. Your mom should have told you that. Or somebody should have told you. . . . If you didn't know that, somebody should have told you that. You got to understand what you're dealing with. If you're able to understand what you're . . . dealing with, you can deal with it. And you simply deal with it. And you can be successful at it. So that's all.

Here, Richard elucidates the strategy that helps him display an unemotional demeanor. Categorizing the occupational arena—and the interactions that occur within it—as a game with rules that can be learned and followed allows him to avoid emotional investment. As a result, he suggests that being too involved and taking workplace issues personally creates a "loser mentality." Thus, Richard shows how his systematic dissection of the interactions that occur in the workplace helps him remain emotionally detached when racial issues occur.

The responses given here indicate divergent emotion work on the part of black professional men that builds on what we know from the existing literature. Though there is very little research on race and its role in shaping emotional performance, data that do exist suggest tokenism may lead to stress and self-hatred. However, research grounded in the emotion work literature indicates that race can influence workplace emotion management and that black men in particular may be loath to show anger as a consequence of the pervasive imagery of the angry black man.[38] In this study, the emotion work of some of the black male respondents reveals that they are more comfortable showing anger than prior studies indicate, whereas the emotion work of other respondents has them displaying feelings of detachment and disinterest in the face of perceived racism.

Summary

In this chapter, I examine black professional men's engagement in emotional performance. Within the framework of emotion management, these men generally report two types of emotion work—showing feelings of anger despite the backdrop of the angry black man and expressing indifference in the face of racial issues. Unlike existing research on tokens and race, which suggests that we might expect to see stress, self-hatred, or the curtailing of anger, this study indicates that black professional men employ other types of emotion management in these contexts. I argue that this is a function of the partial tokenization these men encounter in their work environments.

My previous research on black professionals focused on both men and women in a variety of occupational contexts. In this study, the emphasis on black men in male-dominated positions has yielded different findings about black men's emotional performance. I expect that as a result of partial tokenization, black men are more able to express feelings of anger. In male-dominated jobs in which black men have an easier time bonding with both black and white male colleagues and constructing forms of masculinity that can involve toughness and assertiveness, these minority men may feel more comfortable periodically displaying anger and frustration. However, given the fact that they do not completely assimilate into the work environment, partial tokenization makes them aware of how their racial minority status shapes their work experience. They see that there are different opportunities for networking and mentorship available to them compared with their white male colleagues, keeping them mindful of the inequities they share with women coworkers and, most important here, reminding them to steer clear of the angry black man image. Consequently, the partial tokenization these men encounter may explain why they are more likely to show emotions of anger and frustration, even as they are cognizant that these feelings should not be given free rein. Also, partial tokenization demonstrates that the gendering of occupations shapes how workers of color engage in emotion work. The masculine occupations in which these men are employed help create a level of comfort that facilitates expressions of anger and irritation that black men in other jobs feel are anathema.

In addition, partial tokenization helps explain black men's emotion work of indifference and unconcern. Though black professional men themselves cite easier pathways to acceptance, inclusion, and occupational success than their female counterparts of all races, they still perceive racial discrimination. Thus, even though they may be able to use gender solidarity as a means of bonding with white male coworkers and supervisors, and even though they can develop constructions of masculinity that enable them to cope with stereotyped assumptions, they nevertheless feel confronted with challenges that are related to their position as professional black men. Though, relative to women, some may feel they have an easier time advancing in male-dominated fields, this is not to suggest that they can do so without any problems or obstacles. Consequently, when facing issues that they believe are racially motivated, some black professional men respond with emotion management and show feelings of indifference and detachment.

Conclusion

I began (and titled) this book with a reference to Ralph Ellison's classic novel *Invisible Man*. Though I did not begin the research or this book with a title in mind, I expected to find some aspects of invisibility among the men in my sample. These black professional men's work experiences are relatively invisible in the discipline of sociology (particularly in the research that examines race, gender, work, and occupations). Thus, I expected to learn that these men felt generally marginalized and overlooked in their professions. Instead, their responses reveal a more complicated, nuanced picture—one that includes experiences with discrimination, racism, and stereotyping but also shows relative ease forging relationships with white men, a sense of affinity and connection with other black professional men, and, often, a level of appreciation for the challenges facing women in their professions.

Using the theories of tokenism, gendered organizations/occupations, and intersectionality, along with empirical studies on black professionals, I argue that black men's work experiences cannot be neatly categorized by the existing research. While they are in the minority in their workplaces, their gendered occupations, coupled with the intersections of race, class, and gender, permit them to avoid the tokenization that is often used to frame the occupational experiences of black professional workers. Instead, these men encounter partial tokenization that shapes their relationships with white and black male colleagues and women of all races in the work environment. This partial tokenism also influences the stereotyped informal roles they encounter, the performances of masculinity they construct, as well as the emotion management that becomes necessary in these jobs.

The findings in this study have implications for several other areas of research. In the following sections, I discuss the contributions this study makes to the theory of tokenism, the research on gender interactions in the workplace, and the literature on black professionals. In addition, I make the case for future research in these areas and the implications this study has for public policy.

Token Theory

Though the theory of tokenism provided the original framework I expected to use to analyze these men's experiences, I quickly learned it was not an accurate fit for what my respondents described. There were too many ways in which tokenism did not capture their interactions, emotional performances, and perceptions and attitudes about their positions in their respective occupations. Though Rosabeth Moss Kanter claimed otherwise, subsequent research has largely shown that the theory of tokenism as originally conceived can help explain aspects of white women's experiences in predominantly white male work environments, but it does not always hold true when those conditions are changed.[1] This study shows that considering the race, gender, and class of the token, along with the occupation in which he or she is employed, can create a wholly different experience of being in the numerical minority.

Consequently, this research represents both a theoretical and empirical departure from Kanter's theory of tokenization and offers a different theoretical approach that is intended to capture the complexities of black professional men's work experiences and how these stem from intersections of race, gender, and class.[2] The theory of partial tokenization explains cases in which black professional men, while still in the minority in white male–dominated jobs, may have more success and opportunities for advancement than their female counterparts of all races. To take corporate America as one example, so far, Kenneth Chenault and Stanley O'Neill, both black males, have headed major financial institutions (American Express and Merrill Lynch, respectively) despite the fact that Wall Street has historically been a white male–dominated sector. Conversely, a woman has yet to hold such a lofty job, and reports of institutionalized and widespread sexism are still present.[3] The theory of partial tokenization can help explain why certain male-dominated jobs can prove more open to racial integration and the inclusion of minority men than women of any racial group.

Of course, this appears to be true for professional occupations in particular. As I note in Chapter 3, according to Kris Paap's ethnography of the construction industry, both black men and white women were routinely excluded and marginalized by white men who wanted to retain their status and prestige even as opportunities declined.[4] It would seem that professional, high-status jobs may be more welcoming to minority men than lower-status, skilled jobs in the working class. It is possible that this could change as women and racial minority men continue to make inroads into these occupations, especially if they do so in ways that offset patterns of sex segregation within various subfields.

Additionally, the concept of partial tokenism may be useful for understanding the experiences of other groups in the numerical minority. It may be that workers whose gender alone matches the occupation in which they work are more likely to encounter partial tokenization. Minority women occupied as teachers, for instance, may find that they face barriers within this white female–dominated profession, but the issues they encounter may be more on par with the men in this study. These challenges are also likely shaped by intersections of race, gender, and class such that they are not exact replicas of what the men in this study face.

Gender Interactions

One of the most interesting aspects of this study involves the complicated relationships black professional men say they experience with both black and white women coworkers. Recall that although the token theory suggests that black men's relationships with others in the minority could involve establishing contrasts and emphasizing the differences between themselves and other minority groups, we find only mixed evidence of this among respondents in this study. In some cases, respondents do endorse the idea that women's gender (or race and gender) gives them advantages in the workplace. In other cases, however, black men tend to see evidence of women facing discriminatory or biased treatment and, in some cases, actively take steps to use their own gender privilege to create better opportunities for women workers. Also, some respondents engage in a self-quarantine, in which they seek to isolate themselves from white women colleagues for fear that close interactions might be misread through the lens of racial and gendered stereotypes regarding black male aggression and white female vulnerability. These findings form the basis for my argument that partial tokenization is a more appropriate framework for understanding black professional men's interactions with women colleagues.

These findings also suggest several important directions for future research. The results of this study underscore the paucity of literature that examines cross-gender, cross-racial interactions among groups in various occupations. Thus, future studies should continue to explore the specific parameters of the interactions and occupational relationships that exist among various minorities in work settings. Among other groups, do numerical minorities see one another as allies? Do these groups perceive one another as benefiting from personal characteristics rather than professional qualifications?

Future studies should also pay attention to how gendered occupations shape cross-racial and cross-gender relationships. In this research, I found examples of black men who acknowledged the additional hardships women face in male-dominated jobs and who took steps to address them. However, in my previous research on black men in the nursing field, this sentiment—and the attendant actions to rectify it—were not reported.[5] It is likely that comparing gendered occupations reveals the specific impact these jobs have on different numerical minorities within. Specifically, in a predominantly white female job like nursing, black men would be less likely to classify it as a "masculine" field in which women face challenges because of the gendered dynamics of the job. This might explain the differences in the ways black male nurses versus black male doctors, lawyers, bankers, and engineers develop a sense of solidarity with and connection to women colleagues. How an occupation is gendered, then, may affect the relationships among different types of minority groups within the field.

Additional research might also consider the consequences and implications of the solidarity that does exist between black men and their women colleagues. Existing studies that examine racism suggest that among whites, working-class white women may be the most likely allies to people of color because they can connect the presence and impact of racism to their lived experiences with sexism.[6] Indeed, Peggy McIntosh's classic critique of white privilege stems from her attempts to understand this phenomenon in more detail based on her own frustrating experiences with well-intentioned men who still engage in sexism and are often paternalistically indifferent to women's studies.[7] These authors suggest that white working-class women can therefore potentially be allies in efforts to undermine racial inequality.

The results of this research suggest that parallel arguments may apply to black professional men, particularly when employed in certain jobs. In other words, these men's experience with partial tokenization gives them particular insight into the obstacles women face; therefore, black men may be important supporters in attempts to challenge and end sexism. Indeed, as I document in Chapter 3, we see cases in which black men actively take steps to undermine gender bias and sexism in their workplaces. This makes them potentially valuable partners in the push for male-female equity in the workplace. In fact, the relative ease with which black men describe forging relationships with white male supervisors and colleagues means they may be uniquely situated to help alleviate gender bias in "masculine" jobs.

Yet, while black men display a sense of solidarity with their female colleagues, relationships with other men are uniquely shaped by intersections of race, gender, and class. As shown in Chapter 4, black men form relationships with white male colleagues and supervisors through specific gendered and classed practices—they work out together at the gym, enjoy certain sports together, or at minimum, bank on the sheer numbers of white men in their jobs to locate an ally. Race, gender, and class also shape the level and type of solidarity among black men. While these respondents feel a real sense of camaraderie with other black professional men, this does not necessarily extend to black working-class or working-poor men, particularly those who might be considered part of the underclass.

Ironically, while black men's interactions with women suggest possibilities for countering sexism, black men's more comfortable relationships with white men and other black professional men, along with their social (and presumably physical) distance from black working-poor men, may have very different implications for combating racism. Many of the respondents note that they still face challenges at work and that their assimilation process is far from seamless or perfect, but they still are able to bond relatively easily with other professional men. These bonds, along with a lack of serious ties to working-class or working-poor black men, could distance black professional men from the structural challenges that constrain lower-class black men. Hypothetically, this may undermine cross-class solidarity within black communities and hinder efforts to ameliorate racism across the board.

There have been cases in which well-known black men have been publicly critical of the broader black community. There is Bill Cosby and his vehement 2004 remarks denouncing urban blacks (referenced in the Introduction) for what he perceived as their failure to live up to the ideals set by the civil rights movement. And during his campaign for the presidency, Barack Obama gave a widely referenced Father's Day speech in which he chastised black men for failing to take more responsibility for their children.[8] In other cases, Obama has emphasized the need for black men to exercise individual agency in striving for upward mobility, particularly by placing a higher priority on education, employment, and personal comportment.[9] While these are undoubtedly laudatory goals, it is telling that Obama directs his remarks specifically to black men and does not see the need to lecture white men similarly. In so doing, Obama overtly sends a message that black men *in particular* need to improve their parenting, work, and academic skills. Further, this image of black men as absent fathers with spotty employment records and educations is one often associated with working-class and working-poor black men more so than their professional counterparts.[10]

However, some of the stereotypes that undergird these statements are skewed. For example, despite the widespread stereotype of the absent black father, data show that black nonresident fathers are more likely to visit their children weekly than fathers of other racial groups.[11] Also, according to sociological research, black men's tendency to be overrepresented among the ranks of the unemployed or underemployed is in part a result of occupational practices that actually enhance whites' position in the labor market at the expense of black men. Devah Pager's groundbreaking work in this area shows that white men with criminal records are more likely to receive job callbacks than black men with high school diplomas and no criminal past, and Deirdre Royster's work documents that social networks in vocational jobs favor white men and exclude black men.[12] Finally, Ann Arnett Ferguson demonstrates that white public school teachers preemptively treat black boys as discipline problems, contributing to some of the challenges they face in the educational system.[13] Thus, according to social science data, the social problems that Obama attributes to black men's lack of agency, initiative, and personal traits are more concretely linked to systemic processes facilitating some of these trends.

Hypothetically, Barack Obama could serve as an example of the disconnect that exists between the black professional male and his working-class counterpart. In Obama's ascent to the U.S. Senate and eventually the presidency, he shares similarities with some of the men I interviewed for this study. With his prestigious law degree and training in the legal field, Obama, like many of my respondents, may have found that gender solidarity eased his ability to develop connections with his white male peers as he drew critical social support from black male peers. However, if he has simultaneously maintained a sense of disconnectedness from working-class or working-poor black men, this distance could render him more susceptible to the myths and generalizations he attributes to these men in his Father's Day speech. It is not difficult to imagine that without close ties to working-class or working-poor black men, Obama might perceive the stereotypes to be true and lose sight of the particular ways systemic racism affects black men on the lower end of the economic scale.

Clearly, the men in my sample lack the influence, power, and visibility that Obama has. However, I present Obama's remarks to illustrate the broad consequences of the disconnection black professional men feel in relation to their working-class counterparts. While many respondents identify a sense of solidarity with female counterparts and with other black professional men, this cohesion was markedly absent when it came to black men who did not share their occupational status. Thus, ironically, black professional men might *not* be strong allies in the push to eradicate types of racism that particularly affect minorities in the working and lower classes.

Future research in this area, then, should consider the cross-class relationships between black men and the implications these relationships have. These studies should also consider how the gendering of occupations may matter in developing these relationships. For instance, my research on black male nurses reveals that part of how these men demonstrate masculinity involves emphasizing their status within the broader black community—in particular, working to minimize racial health disparities and venturing into poorer, traditionally underserved black communities.[14] Thus, while black male nurses' cross-class relationships involve efforts to uplift and improve, black male doctors (as well as lawyers, bankers, and engineers) describe cross-class relationships characterized by distance and detachment. Additional research that offers a comparative analysis between black men in "feminine" and "masculine" jobs can assess in more detail how working in these sorts of jobs affects black men's cross-class relationships with other black men.

Finally, this research gives rise to future studies of masculinity, particularly masculinities among marginalized men. I show in Chapter 5 that black professional men are subjected to gender and racially specific informal roles and that they develop marginalized masculinities to counter these depictions. This finding adds to the literature on the types of masculinity among men of color, which is rather scant. However, it leaves room for further research into the connections between work, particularly men's work in gendered occupations, and the performance of masculinity. Part of Raewyn Connell's argument rests on the case that masculinities are relational, so comparative research analyzing minority men's performances of masculinity relative to one another and to white men is necessary to further explicate this subject.[15]

Black Professionals

The research in this book also has important implications for the literature that examines black professional workers. Perhaps most significantly, it underscores the variance among their experiences. Numerous studies have documented the general challenges these workers encounter in predominantly white work settings—the marginalization, the sense of isolation, the hostile treatment from white colleagues.[16] Intersections of race and gender, along with the gendered occupations in which black professionals work, reveal that these challenges are differently experienced among black workers.

Future studies, then, might consider the professions in which black workers are employed. Black women professionals in feminized jobs, for instance, may encounter some dynamics that parallel what I have described here among black professional men. Specifically, they may be able to forge ties to their white female counterparts with relative ease and also feel a sense of empathy with the struggles black men face in the workplace. While additional research is necessary to determine this for certain, the results of this study indicate that gendered jobs—and the gender of the worker—can make a difference in terms of how marginalization and isolation are experienced among black professional employees.

More broadly, the findings from this book also point to the need for more research on black men professionals in general. Much of the literature that focuses on black professional workers either fails to consider gender differences between black men and women or focuses specifically on how race and gender interact to create particular experiences for black professional women.[17] The specific work lives of black professional men are easily lost in this bifurcated analysis. Though there has been a great deal of theoretical and empirical research over the past few decades emphasizing how race and gender intersect to shape various groups' lived experiences in a number of contexts, the literature on black professionals has been slow to reflect this.

One of the most important findings from this study—and a finding that points to the need for continued research on the specific experiences of black men in professional occupations—involves the very interesting claim made by several respondents that because of the gendered advantages of being men in "masculine" jobs, they are sometimes better able to navigate or at least minimize race-related challenges that arise. As Michael, the engineering professor, notes, by sheer numbers, black professionals are likely to find another male who can serve as a mentor and provide the necessary guidance and leadership for success in their chosen field. As I discuss in Chapter 4, contrasts between black men and their white male peers largely takes the form of black workers having inadequate access to critical social networks rather than white colleagues overtly attempting to highlight the differences between the two groups. Thus, a focus on black male professionals—rather than black professionals in general—reveals that in certain occupations, these men may be uniquely situated to take advantage of opportunities for mentorship and guidance that are key to upward mobility.

Paradoxically, this study shows that while partial tokenization gives black men access to important opportunities for mentorship, some very real challenges still confront these men. By focusing on emotional performance, this research highlights some of the ways that black men engage in emotion management and underscores an often overlooked aspect of black professionals' work experiences. My results show that while some black professional men do not completely withhold anger as a way of avoiding the stereotype of the angry black man, others do emotion work that has them favoring the display of indifference over irritation when confronted with racial bias. Some studies of emotion work touch on the connections between emotional performance and health, although without an explicit connection to racial, gender, and occupational status.[18] I would suggest that future studies consider black men's emotion work of exhibiting disinterest in place of anger and the consequences of this for their health and well-being. In light of research that shows that black professional men are likely to have higher rates of hypertension than other groups, it is worth considering whether their emotion management in occupational contexts is a potential causative factor.[19]

Policy Implications

The policy initiative that is by far the most directly aimed at increasing the numbers of black professionals in the contemporary American workplace is affirmative action. First used by President John F. Kennedy in 1961, federal contractors were instructed to "take *affirmative action* to ensure that applicants are employed, and that employees are treated during employment, without regard to their race, creed, color, or national origin" (emphasis added).[20] Although, since that time, affirmative action has become policy in some educational and occupational arenas, it has undergone numerous court challenges. The most recent Supreme Court challenge to affirmative action came in 2009, when seventeen white (and one Latino) firefighters sued the city of New Haven, Connecticut, alleging reverse discrimination when the city sought to comply with existing affirmative action guidelines.

In addition to the court cases, there has been much analysis of the effects and consequences of affirmative action policies. Urban sociologist William Julius Wilson has argued that as established, the benefits of affirmative action are reaped primarily by middle- and upper-class black Americans and that it does nothing to help those that he deems "the truly disadvantaged"—blacks in the underclass who are socially and spatially isolated from mainstream social, employment, and educational centers.[21] Other sociologists have argued that because of the ongoing discrimination faced by black professionals, affirmative action has the potential to provide a necessary corrective to everyday practices of hiring within networks and the like that can reproduce racial inequities in professional settings.[22]

The results of this study show that for black professional men, race still matters in shaping their employment experiences as it creates partial tokenization. Further, the findings indicate that race matters in complex ways—it intersects with gender to inform black men's relationships with other men, with women, with masculinity, and even with their emotional performances. Significantly, these processes, as I describe in this book, are not necessarily ones best rectified by affirmative action as it is currently proscribed. In the case of partially tokenized black men, who can relatively easily form ties to white male colleagues and supervisors, affirmative action may not be the critical factor that lands them a job for which they are well qualified and well prepared. Black men whose partial tokenization offers them the visibility to highlight their skills and accomplishments may find affirmative action is not what ensures their upward mobility. For these black men, the policy may be less effective than originally intended.

Again, I must stress that this is *not* to suggest that black professional men are able to completely avoid challenges and obstacles within their occupations. Rather, I am making the case that the issues facing black professional men are ones that are not necessarily solved by affirmative action in its current form. The paradigm of partial tokenization is meant to convey that the hardships black professional men face are complex and shaped by intersecting factors that reflect both their gender privilege and racial disadvantage. Thus, affirmative action in the workplace is not likely to address the issues that these men point to as some of the biggest challenges shaping their professional careers: namely, the racialized and classed social ties that make their professional networks less efficacious than those of their white male counterparts, or the informal roles that guide colleagues' and supervisors' assessments of their skills and performance. Affirmative action policies will likely not alleviate Welton's feeling that he, as a black male doctor, is subject to the review board when nurses question his methodology, whereas his white colleagues face review only in cases that involve fatalities. Affirmative action also will not address attorney Woody's belief that he is held to a higher standard of professionalism than his white colleagues, who, unlike him, can dress casually at work without drawing attention to themselves or calling their judgment into question. Affirmative action is designed to promote entry. By virtue of hard work, social and economic capital, and ambition, these men have gained entry to their professions of choice. Affirmative action does not address the issues they face past that point.

The challenges these men describe—and the limited role affirmative action can play in addressing them—may well point to the embedment of racial imagery and ideology and the fact that these factors are inextricably ingrained in the cultural imagination and everyday processes. How does social policy erase the presence of informal roles that, despite being grounded in stereotypes, manage to influence workers' interactions? How does policy help black male doctors avoid the indignity of racial slurs when they attempt to care for white patients—or, more important, enable them to avoid the emotion work of showing feelings of indifference in response? Sociologist Cecilia Ridgeway argues that part of the reason gender inequality persists is that when faced with unfamiliar situations, people resort to traditional ideas about gender to explain and make sense of the experience.[23] A similar argument could well be made for black professional men; unfortunately, however, this explanation would still suggest that the use of racialized imagery will persist at least to some extent in influencing occupational outcomes.

I began this project because I was curious about and dismayed by the lack of sociological research that explored how intersections of race and gender affected black men in professional positions. I hope readers come away from this book with an understanding of the complicated, nuanced ways these factors overlap to shape black men's work lives and how they differ from those of their black female counterparts. Partial tokenization offers black men certain opportunities, but it also creates particular challenges. As black men continue to maintain a presence in professional occupations, it is important to consider the specifics of their work experiences and how these experiences can be made more equitable.

Appendix

My data collection for this project involved intensive interviews with forty-two black men: thirteen lawyers, twelve doctors, ten engineers, and seven bankers. I also spoke with a handful of white male professionals ($n = 4$) to get a sense of (1) their experiences in these fields and (2) whether the challenges, obstacles, and issues they perceived in their jobs were different from those of their black male counterparts. Respondents ranged in age from thirty-three to sixty. All had graduated from college. The lawyers and doctors held professional degrees (JDs and MDs, respectively). Four of the ten engineers held doctorates, and two of the remaining six were working on their postgraduate degrees. Two of the bankers held MBAs.

I located respondents through a snowball sample, asking people I knew personally and through professional contacts to refer me to black men who fit the criteria for the study. Interviews generally took place at my office, at the respondent's office, or at a neutral location, such as a coffee shop or bookstore. Whenever respondents consented, interviews were tape-recorded and later transcribed. In the few cases in which respondents did not wish to be recorded, I took detailed notes during the interviews. Most interviews lasted between one and two hours.

I selected intensive interviews as my methodology because they allow respondents to describe in detail various aspects of their occupational experiences. Other studies that attempt to capture the nuances of work in gendered occupations have employed this methodology to great avail, yielding detailed data about different patterns, trends, and practices.[1] This methodology is also common for studies that examine black professionals.[2] In her study of men employed in nontraditional occupations, Christine Williams notes that the intensive interview format enables respondents to clarify comments that might otherwise prove problematic.[3] She also notes that her respondents were able to rephrase statements that she might have perceived as sexist. While I encountered fewer such cases in my interviews, I observed that where respondents did employ this self-correcting technique, they were able to do so without disrupting the flow of the interview.

Typically, I began the intensive interviews with a practice that is fairly common in this methodology: I asked the respondents to share basic demographic information—full names, educational background, where they grew up, and the like.[4] I followed by asking the respondents questions about their relationships with colleagues, the importance of developing close ties with coworkers, how these relationships usually developed, and whether they had ever personally witnessed or heard about tensions between colleagues that were related to issues of race or gender. I then asked the respondents about their relationships with supervisors, their level of job satisfaction, their interest in promotion and advancement, and how they coped with challenges that arose at work.

I structured interview questions to cover a relatively wide array of issues that arise in the workplace in order to create a broad picture of the ways respondents experienced their work environments and to understand, in particular, how men interpreted the challenges they encountered at work, the relationships they developed, and the ways they navigated their occupational terrains. I was careful to frame questions in a way that would not lead respondents in specific directions—questions that did not, for example, assume that issues related to race and gender were salient factors for the men at work. The interview structure allowed respondents to share whether they perceived that issues of race and/or gender surfaced in any way in the workplace. Respondents expressed every view, from the perception that these factors were not obstacles, to the perception that women faced these problems, to the perception that these issues inhibited their own work experiences.

I expect that, as an African American, my own racial status may have helped instill a sense of comfort in respondents. And my status as a professional may have led black male respondents to believe that I might understand and, to an extent, relate to some of the experiences they had faced in predominantly white work settings. Though my gender may have affected my interactions with respondents as well, it did not seem to do so in a way that impaired rapport. Overall, the men in this study seemed comfortable discussing details of their jobs and work experiences.

Data were analyzed using the qualitative software NVivo. I read interview transcripts multiple times and coded data according to themes and concepts that emerged deductively. Thus, themes such as relationships with women, relationships with men, visibility as a helpful or harmful dynamic, and solidarity with or distance from other black men quickly emerged as salient issues for the interviewees.

I should note that in most cases, I followed accepted protocol for qualitative research by editing interview text to eliminate filler words such as "yeah," "um," "like," and "you know" to communicate the speaker's thoughts more clearly. In certain cases, however, I chose to retain instances of "you know." In these cases, I interpreted the phrase as communicating a sense of shared experience—in other words, "you know how it is"—and as adding to, rather than detracting from, our understanding of the speaker's response.

Notes

INTRODUCTION

1. "The Wrong Man," *Washington Post*, June 25, 2006, available at http://www
.washingtonpost.com/wp-dyn/content/article/2006/06/24/AR2006062401082
.html.

2. Todd Clear, *Imprisoning Communities: How Mass Incarceration Makes
Disadvantaged Neighborhoods Worse* (New York: Oxford University Press, 2007);
Ann Arnett Ferguson, *Bad Boys: Public Schools in the Making of Black Masculinity*
(Ann Arbor: University of Michigan Press, 2001); William Julius Wilson, *The
Truly Disadvantaged: The Inner City, the Underclass, and Public Policy* (Chicago:
University of Chicago Press, 1987); Alford Young, *The Minds of Marginalized Black
Men* (Princeton, NJ: Princeton University Press, 2004).

3. "Bill Cosby: Address at the NAACP Fiftieth Anniversary of *Brown v. the
Board of Education*," American Rhetoric, May 17, 2004, available at http://www
.americanrhetoric.com/speeches/billcosbypoundcakespeech.htm.

4. Bureau of Labor Statistics, "Household Data Annual Averages," table 10:
Employed Persons by Occupation, Race, Hispanic, or Latino Ethnicity, and Sex,
2006, available at ftp://ftp.bls.gov/pub/special.requests/lf/aa2006/aat10.txt.

5. Dana Britton, *At Work in the Iron Cage* (New York: New York University
Press, 2003); Maria Charles and David Grusky, *Occupational Ghettos: The Worldwide Segregation of Women and Men* (Stanford, CA: Stanford University Press,
2004); Christine L. Williams, *Still a Man's World: Men Who Do "Women's Work"*
(Berkeley: University of California Press, 1995).

6. Patricia Hill Collins, *Black Feminist Thought: Knowledge, Consciousness, and the Politics of Empowerment* (New York: Routledge), 2000.

7. Rosabeth Moss Kanter, *Men and Women of the Corporation* (New York: Basic Books, 1977).

8. Joan Acker, "Hierarchies, Jobs, Bodies: A Theory of Gendered Organizations," *Gender and Society* 4, no. 2 (1990): 139–158.

9. Kanter, *Men and Women.*

10. Arlie Russell Hochschild, *The Managed Heart: Commercialization of Human Feeling* (Berkeley: University of California Press, 1983); Robin Leidner, *Fast Food, Fast Talk: Service Work and the Routinization of Everyday Life* (Berkeley: University of California Press, 1993); Susan E. Martin, "Police Force or Police Service? Gender and Emotional Labor," *Annals of the American Academy of Political and Social Science* 561, no. 1 (1999): 111–126; Jennifer Pierce, *Gender Trials: Emotional Lives in Contemporary Law Firms* (Berkeley: University of California Press, 1995).

CHAPTER 1

1. Rosabeth Moss Kanter, *Men and Women of the Corporation* (New York: Basic Books, 1977); Joan Acker, "Hierarchies, Jobs, Bodies: A Theory of Gendered Organizations," *Gender and Society* 4, no. 2 (1990): 139–158.

2. Kanter, *Men and Women.*

3. Ibid., 210.

4. Kanter, *Men and Women.*

5. Catherine J. Turco, "Cultural Foundations of Tokenism: Evidence from the Leveraged Buyout Industry," *American Sociological Review* 75, no. 6 (2010): 894–913.

6. Lilian Floge and Deborah M. Merrill, "Tokenism Reconsidered: Male Nurses and Female Physicians in a Hospital Setting," *Social Forces* 64, no. 4 (1986): 925–947; Kanter, *Men and Women.*

7. Floge and Merrill, "Tokenism Reconsidered."

8. Louise M. Roth, *Selling Women Short: Gender Inequality on Wall Street* (Princeton, NJ: Princeton University Press, 2006).

9. Ibid.; Kanter, *Men and Women.*

10. Floge and Merrill, "Tokenism Reconsidered."

11. Susan Antilla, *Tales from the Boom-Boom Room: Women vs. Wall Street* (Princeton, NJ: Bloomberg Press), 2002.

12. Roth, *Selling Women Short*; Kanter, *Men and Women.*

13. Kris Paap, *Working Construction: Why White Working-Class Men Put Themselves and the Labor Movement in Harm's Way* (Ithaca, NY: Cornell University Press, 2006); Kanter, *Men and Women.*

14. Paap, *Working Construction.*

15. Ibid.; Floge and Merrill, "Tokenism Reconsidered"; Roth, *Selling Women Short*; Kanter, *Men and Women.*

16. Floge and Merrill, "Tokenism Reconsidered"; Roth, *Selling Women Short*; Paap, *Working Construction.*

17. Paap, *Working Construction.*

18. Kanter, *Men and Women.*

19. Acker, "Hierarchies, Jobs, Bodies."

20. Kanter, *Men and Women.*

21. Acker, "Hierarchies, Jobs, Bodies."

22. Dana Britton, *At Work in the Iron Cage* (New York: New York University Press, 2003); Kirsten Dellinger, "Maculinities in Safe and Embattled Organizations: Accounting for Pornographic and Feminist Magazines," *Gender and Society* 18, no. 5 (2004): 545–566.

23. Christine L. Williams, *Still a Man's World: Men Who Do "Women's Work"* (Berkeley: University of California Press, 1995).

24. Ibid.; Kanter, *Men and Women.*

25. Floge and Merrill, "Tokenism Reconsidered"; Roth, *Selling Women Short*; Paap, *Working Construction.*

26. Williams, *Still a Man's World.*

27. Kanter, *Men and Women.*

28. Williams, *Still a Man's World.*

29. Kanter, *Men and Women.*

30. Williams, *Still a Man's World.*

31. Kanter, *Men and Women.*

32. Jennifer L. Pierce, *Gender Trials: Emotional Lives in Contemporary Law Firms* (Berkeley: University of California Press, 1995); Williams, *Still a Man's World.*

33. Pierce, *Gender Trials.*

34. Ibid., 1.

35. Ibid.; Williams, *Still a Man's World.*

36. Pierce, *Gender Trials*

37. Ibid.

38. Williams, *Still a Man's World.*

39. Pamela B. Jackson, Peggy A. Thoits, and Howard F. Taylor, "Composition of the Workplace and Psychological Well-Being: The Effects of Tokenism on America's Black Elite," *Social Forces* 74 (1995): 543–557.

40. Ibid.

41. Ibid.

42. Charisse Jones and Kumea Shorter-Gooden, *Shifting: The Double Lives of Black Women in America* (New York: HarperCollins, 2003).

43. Ibid.; Kanter, *Men and Women.*

44. Joe R. Feagin and Melvin P. Sikes, *Living with Racism: The Black Middle-Class Experience* (Boston: Beacon Press, 1995).

45. Vincent Roscigno, *The Faces of Discrimination: How Race and Gender Impact Work and Home Lives* (Lanham, MD: Rowman and Littlefield, 2007).

46. Ibid., 100.

47. Victoria Kaplan, *Structural Inequality: Black Architects in the United States* (Lanham, MD: Rowman and Littlefield, 2006).

48. Sharon M. Collins, *Black Corporate Executives: The Making and Breaking of a Black Middle Class* (Philadelphia: Temple University Press, 1997).

49. Marlese Durr and John R. Logan, "Racial Submarkets in Government Employment," *Sociological Forum* 12 (1997): 353–370.

50. Collins, *Black Corporate Executives*.

51. Ibid.; Durr and Logan, "Racial Submarkets."

52. Jackson, Thoits, and Taylor, "Composition of the Workplace."

53. Kanter, *Men and Women*.

54. Paap, *Working Construction*; Pierce, *Gender Trials*; Roth, *Selling Women Short*; Christine L. Williams, "The Glass Escalator: Hidden Advantages for Men in the Female Professions," *Social Problems* 39, no. 3 (1992): 253–267; Williams, *Still a Man's World*.

55. Adia Harvey Wingfield, "Racializing the Glass Escalator: Reconsidering Men's Experiences with 'Women's Work,'" *Gender and Society* 23, no. 1 (2009): 5–26.

56. Irene Browne and Joya Misra, "The Intersection of Gender and Race in the Labor Market," *Annual Review of Sociology* 29 (2003): 487–513; Ann Arnett Ferguson, *Bad Boys: Public Schools in the Making of Black Masculinity* (Ann Arbor: University of Michigan Press, 2001); Cheryl Townsend Gilkes, "Building in Many Places: Multiple Commitments and Ideologies in Black Women's Community Work," in *Women and the Politics of Empowerment: Perspectives from Communities and Workplaces*, ed. Ann Bookman and Sandra Morgen (Philadelphia: Temple University Press, 1988), 53–76; Jennifer Nelson, *Women of Color and the Reproductive Rights Movement* (New York: New York University Press, 2003).

57. Maxine B. Zinn and Bonnie T. Dill, "Theorizing Differences from Multiracial Feminism," *Feminist Studies* 22, no. 2 (1996): 321–332.

58. For an excellent discussion, see Nelson, *Women of Color*.

59. Joan Acker, *Class Questions, Feminist Answers* (Lanham, MD: Rowman and Littlefield, 2006).

60. Ella L. J. Edmondson Bell and Stella M. Nkomo, *Our Separate Ways: Black and White Women and the Struggle for Professional Identity* (Boston: Harvard Business School Press, 2003).

61. Ibid.

62. Yanick St. Jean and Joe Feagin, *Double Burden: Black Women and Everyday Racism* (Armonk, NY: M. E. Sharpe, 1998).

63. Ibid.; Bell and Nkomo, *Our Separate Ways*; Lynne Weber and Elizabeth Higginbotham, "Perceptions of Workplace Discrimination among Black and White Professional-Managerial Women," in *Latina and African American Women at Work*, ed. Irene Brown (New York: Russell Sage, 1999), 327–353.

64. Paap, *Working Construction*; Williams, "The Glass Escalator"; Williams, *Still a Man's World*; Wingfield, "Racializing the Glass Escalator."

65. Kanter, *Men and Women.*

66. Ibid.; Pierce, *Gender Trials*; Williams, *Still a Man's World.*

CHAPTER 2

1. Joe R. Feagin and Melvin P. Sikes, *Living with Racism: The Black Middle-Class Experience* (Boston: Beacon Press, 1995).

2. Alice Abel Kemp, *Women's Work: Degraded and Devalued* (Englewood Cliffs, NJ: Prentice Hall, 1994).

3. Rosabeth Moss Kanter, *Men and Women of the Corporation* (New York: Basic Books, 1977).

4. Ibid., 212.

5. Ibid., 214.

6. Kanter, *Men and Women.*

7. Ibid.

8. Ibid.

9. Ibid., 215.

10. Ibid., 213.

11. Ibid., 216.

12. Ellis Cose, *The Rage of a Privileged Class* (New York: HarperCollins, 1993); Charisse Jones and Kumea Shorter-Gooden, *Shifting: The Double Lives of Black Women in America* (New York: HarperCollins, 2003).

13. For a detailed discussion of this image, see Patricia Hill Collins, *Black Sexual Politics: African Americans, Gender, and the New Racism* (New York: Routledge, 2004).

14. Kanter, *Men and Women.*

15. Ibid.

16. Jennifer Pierce, *Gender Trials: Emotional Lives in Contemporary Law Firms* (Berkeley: University of California Press, 1995).

17. Feagin and Sikes, *Living with Racism*; Richard L. Zweigenhaft and William G. Domhoff, *Diversity in the Power Elite: How It Happened, Why It Matters* (Lanham, MD: Rowman and Littlefield, 2006).

18. Kanter, *Men and Women.*

19. Ibid.

20. Ibid.

21. Cose, *The Rage.*

22. Ellis Cose, *The End of Anger* (New York: HarperCollins, 2011).

CHAPTER 3

1. Yanick St. Jean and Joe Feagin, *Double Burden: Black Women and Everyday Racism* (Armonk, NY: M. E. Sharpe, 1998), 55.

2. Patricia Hill Collins, *Black Sexual Politics: African Americans, Gender, and the New Racism* (New York: Routledge, 2004), 146.

3. Angela Y. Davis, *Women, Race, and Class* (New York: Basic Books, 1981).

4. Bureau of Labor Statistics, "Household Data Annual Averages," 2006, table 10: Employed Persons by Occupation, Race, Hispanic, or Latino Ethnicity, and Sex," available at ftp://ftp.bls.gov/pub/special.requests/lf/aa2006/aat10.txt.

5. Michael S. Kimmel, "Masculinity as Homophobia: Fear, Shame, and Silence in the Construction of Gender Identity," in *Men and Masculinity: A Text Reader*, ed. Theodore F. Cohen (Belmont, CA: Wadsworth Thomson Learning, 2001), 29–41; Michael S. Kimmel, *Manhood in America: A Cultural History* (New York: Oxford University Press, 2012); Earl Ofari Hutchinson, *The Assassination of the Black Male Image* (New York: Simon and Schuster, 1997).

6. Davis, *Women, Race, and Class*; Lynne Olsen, *Freedom's Daughters: The Unsung Heroines of the Civil Rights Movement from 1830 to 1970* (New York: Scribner, 2001).

7. Adia Harvey Wingfield, "Are Some Emotions Marked 'White Only'? Racialized Feeling Rules in Professional Workplaces," *Social Problems* 57, no. 2 (2010): 251–268.

8. Rosabeth Moss Kanter, *Men and Women of the Corporation* (New York: Basic Books, 1977).

9. Ibid.

10. Ibid., 222.

11. Erving Goffman, *Stigma: Notes on the Management of Spoiled Identity* (New York: Simon and Schuster, 1963).

12. Kanter, *Men and Women*.

13. Ibid., 227.

14. Ibid., 228.

15. Kanter, *Men and Women*.

16. Ibid.

17. Ibid.

18. Kris Paap, *Working Construction: Why White Working-Class Men Put Themselves and the Labor Movement in Harm's Way* (Ithaca, NY: Cornell University Press, 2006).

19. Catherine J. Turco, "Cultural Foundations of Tokenism: Evidence from the Leveraged Buyout Industry," *American Sociological Review* 75, no. 6 (2010): 894–913.

20. Ibid.

21. Kanter, *Men and Women*.

22. Christine L. Williams, *Still a Man's World: Men Who Do "Women's Work"* (Berkeley: University of California Press, 1995).

23. Ella L. J. Edmonson Bell and Stella M. Nkomo, *Our Separate Ways: Black and White Women and the Struggle for Professional Identity* (Boston: Harvard Business School Press, 2003).

24. Turco, "Cultural Foundations."

25. Kanter, *Men and Women*.

26. Michael S. Kimmel, *Guyland: The Perilous World Where Boys Become Men* (New York: Harper, 2008).

27. Paap, *Working Construction.*

28. Ibid.

29. Ibid.

30. Ibid.

31. Ibid.

32. Ibid.

33. Nijole Benokraitis and Joe Feagin, *Modern Sexism: Blatant, Subtle, and Covert Discrimination* (Englewood Cliffs, NJ: Prentice Hall, 1995).

34. Lilian Floge and Deborah M. Merrill, "Tokenism Reconsidered: Male Nurses and Female Physicians in a Hospital Setting," *Social Forces* 64, no. 4 (1986): 925–947.

35. Kanter, *Men and Women.*

36. Bell and Nkomo, *Our Separate Ways*; Charisse Jones and Kumea Shorter-Gooden, *Shifting: The Double Lives of Black Women in America* (New York: HarperCollins, 2003); Mary Texiera Thierry, "'Who Protects and Serves Me?' A Case Study of Sexual Harassment of African American Women in One U.S. Law Enforcement Agency," *Gender and Society* 16, no. 4 (2002): 524–545.

37. Bell and Nkomo, *Our Separate Ways*; St. Jean and Feagin, *Double Burden*; Richard L. Zweigenhaft and William G. Domhoff, *Diversity in the Power Elite: How It Happened, Why It Matters* (Lanham, MD: Rowman and Littlefield, 2006).

38. Kanter, *Men and Women.*

39. Ibid.

40. Ibid.

41. Davis, *Women, Race, and Class.*

42. Kanter, *Men and Women.*

43. Ibid.

44. Joe R. Feagin and Melvin P. Sikes, *Living with Racism: The Black Middle-Class Experience* (Boston: Beacon Press, 1995).

45. Kanter, *Men and Women.*

46. Louise M. Roth, *Selling Women Short: Gender Inequality on Wall Street* (Princeton, NJ: Princeton University Press), 2006.

47. Kanter, *Men and Women.*

48. Ibid.

CHAPTER 4

1. Rosabeth Moss Kanter, *Men and Women of the Corporation* (New York: Basic Books, 1977).

2. Ibid.

3. Ibid., 223.

4. Ibid., 225.

5. Kanter, *Men and Women.*

6. Joe R. Feagin and Melvin P. Sikes, *Living with Racism: The Black Middle-Class Experience* (Boston: Beacon Press, 1995), 167.

7. Kanter, *Men and Women.*

8. Catherine J. Turco, "Cultural Foundations of Tokenism: Evidence from the Leveraged Buyout Industry," *American Sociological Review* 75, no. 6 (2010): 894–913.

9. Kanter, *Men and Women.*

10. Ibid.

11. Ibid.

12. Christine L. Williams, *Still a Man's World: Men Who Do "Women's Work"* (Berkeley: University of California Press, 1995).

13. Ibid.

14. Adia Harvey Wingfield, "Racializing the Glass Escalator: Reconsidering Men's Experiences with 'Women's Work,'" *Gender and Society* 23, no. 1 (2009): 5–26.

15. Kanter, *Men and Women.*

16. Ibid.

17. Jennifer L. Pierce, "Racing for Innocence: Whiteness, Corporate Culture, and the Backlash against Affirmative Action," in *White Out: The Continuing Significance of Racism,* ed. Ashley Doane and Eduardo Bonilla-Silva (New York: Routledge, 2003), 199–214.

18. Pierce, "Racing for Innocence," 211.

19. William Harvey and Eugene Anderson, *Minorities in Higher Education: 21st Annual Status Report* (Washington, DC: American Council of Education, 2005).

20. Kanter, *Men and Women.*

21. Ibid.

22. Ibid., 230.

23. Adia Harvey Wingfield, *Doing Business with Beauty: Black Women, Hair Salons, and the Racial Enclave Economy* (Lanham, MD: Rowman and Littlefield, 2008).

24. Kanter, *Men and Women.*

25. E. Franklin Frazier, *Black Bourgeoisie* (New York: Free Press, 1957); Karyn R. Lacy, *Blue-Chip Black: Race, Class, and Status in the New Black Middle Class* (Berkeley: University of California Press, 2007).

CHAPTER 5

1. Kris Paap, *Working Construction: Why White Working-Class Men Put Themselves and the Labor Movement in Harm's Way* (Ithaca, NY: Cornell University Press, 2006); Jennifer Pierce, *Gender Trials* (Berkeley: University of California Press, 1995); Louise M. Roth, *Selling Women Short: Gender Inequality on Wall Street* (Princeton, NJ: Princeton University Press, 2006).

2. Anthony S. Chen, "Lives at the Center of the Periphery, Lives at the Periphery of the Center," *Gender and Society* 13, no. 5 (1999): 584–607; Adia Harvey Wingfield, "Are Some Emotions Marked 'Whites Only'? Racialized Feeling Rules in Professional Workplaces," *Social Problems* 57, no. 2 (2010): 251–268.

3. Rosabeth Moss Kanter, *Men and Women of the Corporation* (New York: Basic Books, 1997).

4. Ibid.

5. Ibid., 230.

6. Kanter, *Men and Women*.

7. Ibid.

8. Ibid., 232.

9. Ibid., 233.

10. Kanter, *Men and Women*.

11. Ibid.

12. Nijole Benokraitis and Joe Feagin, *Modern Sexism: Blatant, Subtle, and Covert Discrimination* (Englewood Cliffs, NJ: Prentice Hall, 1995), 34.

13. Kanter, *Men and Women*, 237.

14. Kanter, *Men and Women*.

15. For an excellent example of how these advantages for white men accrue in law schools, see Wendy Leo Moore, *Reproducing Racism: White Space, Elite Law Schools, and Racial Inequality* (Lanham, MD: Rowman and Littlefield, 2008).

16. Thomas M. Shapiro, *The Hidden Costs of Being African American: How Wealth Perpetuates Inequality* (New York: Oxford University Press, 2004).

17. Eduardo Bonilla-Silva, *White Supremacy and Racism in the Post–Civil Rights Era* (Denver: Lynne Riemmer Press, 2001); Joe R. Feagin, *Systemic Racism: A Theory of Oppression* (New York: Routledge, 2006).

18. Sharon M. Collins, "The Marginalization of Black Executives," *Social Problems* 36, no. 4 (1989): 317–331.

19. Ibid.

20. Kanter, *Men and Women*.

21. Raewyn W. Connell, "Cool Guys, Swots, and Wimps: The Interplay of Masculinity and Education," *Oxford Review of Education* 15, no. 3 (1989): 291–303.

22. Michael S. Kimmel, "Masculinity as Homophobia: Fear, Shame, and Silence in the Construction of Gender Identity," in *Men and Masculinity: A Text Reader*, ed. Theodore F. Cohen (Belmont, CA: Wadsworth Thomson Learning, 2001); Michael S. Kimmel, *Guyland: The Perilous World Where Boys Become Men* (New York: Harper, 2008).

23. Erving Goffman, *Stigma: Notes on the Management of Spoiled Identity* (New York: Simon and Schuster, 1963), 128.

24. Michael S. Kimmel, *Manhood in America: A Cultural History*. New York: Oxford University Press 2012.

25. Raewyn W. Connell, *Masculinities* (Berkeley: University of California Press, 1995).

26. Kimmel, *Guyland.*

27. C. J. Pascoe, *Dude, You're a Fag! Masculinity and Sexuality in High School* (Berkeley: University of California Press, 2007).

28. Connell, *Masculinities.*

29. Ibid.

30. Chen, "Lives at the Center."

31. Richard Majors and Janet M. Billson, *Cool Pose: The Dilemmas of Black Manhood in America* (New York: Lexington Books, 1992).

32. Chen, "Lives at the Center."

33. Michele Lamont, *The Dignity of Working Men: Morality and the Boundaries of Race, Class, and Immigration* (Cambridge, MA: Harvard University Press, 2000).

34. Lamont, *The Dignity*, 47.

35. Wingfield, "Are Some Emotions Marked 'Whites Only'?"

36. Paap, *Working Construction*; Pierce, *Gender Trials.*

37. Kanter, *Men and Women.*

38. Ibid.

39. For examples of these behaviors in the legal field, see Pierce, *Gender Trials.*

40. Kanter, *Men and Women.*

41. Ibid.

42. Chen, "Lives at the Center"; Wingfield, "Are Some Emotions Marked 'Whites Only'?"

43. Kirsten Dellinger, "Masculinities in Safe and Embattled Organizations: Accounting for Pornographic and Feminist Magazines," *Gender and Society* 18, no. 5 (2004): 545–566; Ann Arnett Ferguson, *Bad Boys: Public Schools and the Making of Black Masculinity* (Ann Arbor: University of Michigan Press, 2001).

44. Joe R. Feagin and Melvin P. Sikes, *Living with Racism: The Black Middle-Class Experience* (Boston: Beacon Press, 1995); Pamela B. Jackson, Peggy A. Thoits, and Howard F. Taylor, "Composition of the Workplace and Psychological Well-Being: The Effects of Tokenism on America's Black Elite," *Social Forces* 74 (1995): 543–557; Richard L. Zweigenhaft and William G. Domhoff, *Diversity in the Power Elite: How It Happened, Why It Matters* (Lanham, MD: Rowman and Littlefield, 2006).

45. Ella L. J. Edmondson Bell and Stella M. Nkomo, *Our Separate Ways: Black and White Women and the Struggle for Professional Identity* (Boston: Harvard Business School Press, 2003); Roxana Harlow, "'Race Doesn't Matter, But . . .': The Effect of Race on Professors' Experiences and Emotion Management in the Undergraduate College Classroom," *Social Psychology Quarterly* 66, no. 4 (2003): 348–363.

CHAPTER 6

1. Ellis Cose, *The Rage of a Privileged Class* (New York: HarperCollins, 1993).

2. Ibid., 1.

3. Cose, *The Rage.*

4. Ellis Cose, *The End of Anger* (New York: HarperCollins, 2011).

5. Ibid., 12.

6. Cose, *The End of Anger*.

7. Ibid.; Cose, *The Rage*.

8. Rosabeth Moss Kanter, *Men and Women of the Corporation* (New York: Basic Books, 1977).

9. Ibid., 240.

10. Kanter, *Men and Women*.

11. Arlie Russell Hochschild, *The Managed Heart: Commercialization of Human Feeling* (Berkeley: University of California Press, 1983).

12. Ibid.

13. Ibid.

14. Ibid.

15. Robin Leidner, *Fast Food, Fast Talk: Service Work and the Routinization of Everyday Life* (Berkeley: University of California Press, 1993); Kathryn Lively, "Client Contact and Emotional Labor: Upsetting the Balance and Evening the Field," *Work and Occupations* 29, no. 2 (2002): 198–225; Jennifer Pierce, *Gender Trials* (Berkeley: University of California Press, 1995); Steven H. Lopez, "Emotional Labor and Organized Emotional Care: Conceptualizing Nursing Home Care Work," *Work and Occupations* 33, no. 2 (2006): 133–160.

16. Hochschild, *The Managed Heart*.

17. Ibid.

18. Ibid.

19. Ibid.

20. Kiran Mirchandani, "Challenging Racial Silences in Studies of Emotion Work: Contributions from Anti-racist Feminist Theory," *Organization Studies* 24, no. 5 (2003): 721–742.

21. Pierce, *Gender Trials*.

22. Yen Le Espiritu, *Asian American Women and Men: Labor, Laws, and Love* (Thousand Oaks, CA: Russell Sage Publications, 1996).

23. Ibid.

24. Miliann Kang, "The Managed Hand: The Commercialization of Bodies and Emotions in Korean Immigrant–Owned Nail Salons," *Gender and Society* 17 (2003): 820–839; Miliann Kang, *The Managed Hand: Race, Gender, and the Body in Beauty Service Work* (Berkeley: University of California Press, 2010).

25. Kang, "The Managed Hand"; Kang, *The Managed Hand*.

26. Kang, "The Managed Hand"; Kang, *The Managed Hand*.

27. Kang, "The Managed Hand"; Kang, *The Managed Hand*.

28. Roxana Harlow, "'Race Doesn't Matter, But . . .': The Effect of Race on Professors' Experiences and Emotion Management in the Undergraduate College Classroom," *Social Psychology Quarterly* 66, no. 4 (2003): 348–363.

29. Harlow, "'Race Doesn't Matter'"; Kang, "The Managed Hand."

30. Adia Harvey Wingfield, "Are Some Emotions Marked 'Whites Only'? Racialized Feeling Rules in Professional Workplaces," *Social Problems* 57, no. 2 (2010): 251–268.

31. Kanter, *Men and Women*.

32. Wingfield, "Are Some Emotions Marked 'Whites Only'?" 259.

33. Ibid., 262.

34. Pamela B. Jackson, Peggy A. Thoits, and Howard F. Taylor, "Composition of the Workplace and Psychological Well-Being: The Effects of Tokenism on America's Black Elite," *Social Forces* 74 (1995): 543–557.

35. Wingfield, "Are Some Emotions Marked 'Whites Only'?" 265.

36. Kang, "The Managed Hand"; Kang, *The Managed Hand*; Harlow, "'Race Doesn't Matter.'"

37. Kanter, *Men and Women*; Wingfield, "Are Some Emotions"; Kang, "The Managed Hand"; Kang, *The Managed Hand*.

38. Kanter, *Men and Women*; Harlow, "'Race Doesn't Matter'"; Kang, "The Managed Hand"; Kang, *The Managed Hand*; Wingfield, "Are Some Emotions Marked 'Whites Only'?"

CONCLUSION

1. Rosabeth Moss Kanter, *Men and Women of the Corporation* (New York: Basic Books, 1977); Lilian Floge and Deborah M. Merrill, "Tokenism Reconsidered: Male Nurses and Female Physicians in a Hospital Setting," *Social Forces* 64, no. 4 (1986): 925–947; Jennifer L. Pierce, *Gender Trials: Emotional Lives in Contemporary Law Firms* (Berkeley: University of California Press, 1995); Christine L. Williams, *Still a Man's World: Men Who Do Women's Work* (Berkeley: University of California Press, 1995).

2. Kanter, *Men and Women*.

3. Ron Susskind, *Confidence Men* (New York: HarperCollins, 2011).

4. Kris Paap, *Working Construction: Why White Working-Class Men Put Themselves and the Labor Movement in Harm's Way* (Ithaca, NY: Cornell University Press), 2006.

5. Adia Harvey Wingfield, "Racializing the Glass Escalator: Reconsidering Men's Experiences with 'Women's Work,'" *Gender and Society* 23, no. 1 (2009): 5–26.

6. Eduardo Bonilla-Silva, *White Supremacy and Racism in the Post–Civil Rights Era* (Denver: Lynne Riemmer Press, 2001); Ruth Frankenberg, *White Women, Race Matters: The Social Construction of Whiteness* (Minneapolis: University of Minnesota Press, 1993).

7. Peggy McIntosh, "White Privilege and Male Privilege: A Personal Account of Coming to See Correspondences through Work in Women's Studies," in *Race, Class, and Gender: An Anthology*, ed. Margaret L. Andersen and Patricia Hill Collins, 2nd ed. (Belmont, CA: Wadsworth, 1995), 76–87.

8. "Obama's Father's Day Speech," CNN, June 28, 2008, available at http://articles.cnn.com/2008-06-27/politics/obama.fathers.ay_1_foundation-black-children-rock?_s=PM:POLITICS.

9. Adia Harvey Wingfield and Joe Feagin, *Yes We Can? White Racial Framing and the 2008 Presidential Campaign* (Lanham, MD: Rowman and Littlefield, 2009).

10. Joleen Kirschenman and Kathryn M. Neckerman, "'We'd Love to Hire Them, But . . .': The Meaning of Race for Employers," in *The Urban Underclass*, ed. Christopher Jencks and Paul E. Peterson (Washington, DC: Brookings Institution, 1991), 203–232.

11. R. Lerman and E. Sorenson, "Father Involvement with Their Nonmarital Children: Patterns, Determinants, and Effects on Their Earnings," *Marriage and Family Review* 29 (2000): 137–158.

12. Devah Pager, *Marked: Race, Crime, and Finding Work in an Era of Mass Incarceration* (Chicago: University of Chicago Press, 2007); Deirdre A. Royster, *Race and the Invisible Hand: How White Networks Exclude Black Men from Blue-Collar Jobs* (Berkeley: University of California Press, 2003).

13. Ann Arnett Ferguson, *Bad Boys: Public Schools and the Making of Black Masculinity* (Ann Arbor: University of Michigan Press, 2001).

14. Adia Harvey Wingfield, "Are Some Emotions Marked 'Whites Only'? Racialized Feeling Rules in Professional Workplaces," *Social Problems* 57, no. 2 (2010): 251–268.

15. Raewyn W. Connell, *Masculinities* (Berkeley: University of California Press, 1995).

16. Ella L. J. Bell and Stella M. Nkomo, *Our Separate Ways: Black and White Women and the Struggle for Professional Identity* (Boston: Harvard Business School Press, 2003); Ellis Cose, *The Rage of a Privileged Class* (New York: HarperCollins, 1993); Joe R. Feagin and Melvin P. Sikes, *Living with Racism: The Black Middle-Class Experience* (Boston: Beacon Press, 1995); Lynne Weber and Elizabeth Higginbotham, "Black and White Professional-Managerial Women's Perceptions of Racism and Sexism in the Workplace," in *Women and Work: Exploring Race, Ethnicity, and Class*, vol. 6, ed. Elizabeth Higginbotham and Mary Romero (Thousand Oaks, CA: Russell Sage, 1997), 153–175.

17. Cose, *The Rage*; Yanick St. Jean and Joe Feagin, *Double Burden: Black Women and Everyday Racism* (Armonk, NY: M. E. Sharpe, 1998).

18. Amy Wharton, "The Psychosocial Consequences of Emotional Labor," *Annals of the American Academy of Political and Social Science* 561, no. 1 (1995): 158–176.

19. National Center for Health Statistics, *Health, United States, 2008* (Washington, DC: U.S. Government Printing Office, 2009), pp. 1–589, available at http://www.cdc.gov/nchs/data/hus/hus08.pdf.

20. U.S. Equal Employment Opportunity Commission, Executive Order 10925, March 6, 1961, available at http://www.eeoc.gov/eeoc/history/35th/thelaw/eo-10925.html.

21. William Julius Wilson, *The Truly Disadvantaged: The Inner City, the Underclass, and Public Policy* (Chicago: University of Chicago Press, 1987).

22. Michael Brown, Martin Carnoy, Elliott Currie, Troy Duster, David B. Oppenheimer, Marjorie Shultz, and David Wellman, *Whitewashing Race: The Myth of a Color-Blind Society* (Berkeley: University of California Press, 2003); Joe R. Feagin, *Racist America: Roots, Current Realities, and Future Reparations*, 2nd ed.

(New York: Routledge, 2010); Kirschenman and Neckerman, "'We'd Love to Hire Them, But . . .'"

23. Cecilia Ridgeway, *Framed by Gender: How Gender Inequality Persists in the Modern World* (New York: Oxford University Press, 2011).

APPENDIX

1. Dana Britton, *At Work in the Iron Cage* (New York: New York University Press, 2003); Christine L. Williams, *Still a Man's World: Men Who Do "Women's Work"* (Berkeley: University of California Press, 1995).

2. See, for example, Ellis Cose, *The Rage of a Privileged Class* (New York: HarperCollins, 1993); and Joe R. Feagin and Melvin P. Sikes, *Living with Racism: The Black Middle-Class Experience* (Boston: Beacon Press, 1995).

3. Williams, *Still a Man's World.*

4. Bruce L. Berg, *Qualitative Research Methods for Social Sciences,* 6th ed. (Boston: Pearson, 2007).

Bibliography

Acker, Joan. "Hierarchies, Jobs, Bodies: A Theory of Gendered Organizations." *Gender and Society* 4, no. 2 (1990): 139–158.

Antilla, Susan. *Tales from the Boom-Boom Room: Women vs. Wall Street.* Princeton, NJ: Bloomberg Press, 2002.

Bell, Ella L. J. Edmondson, and Stella M. Nkomo. *Our Separate Ways: Black and White Women and the Struggle for Professional Identity.* Boston: Harvard Business School Press, 2003.

Benokraitis, Nijole, and Joe Feagin. *Modern Sexism: Blatant, Subtle, and Covert Discrimination.* Englewood Cliffs, NJ: Prentice Hall, 1995.

Berg, Bruce L. *Qualitative Research Methods for Social Sciences.* 6th ed. Boston: Pearson, 2007.

"Bill Cosby: Address at the NAACP Fiftieth Anniversary of *Brown v. the Board of Education.*" American Rhetoric, May 17, 2004. Available at http://www .americanrhetoric.com/speeches/billcosbypoundcakespeech.htm.

Bonilla-Silva, Eduardo. *White Supremacy and Racism in the Post–Civil Rights Era.* Denver: Lynne Riemmer Press, 2001.

Britton, Dana. *At Work in the Iron Cage.* New York: New York University Press, 2003.

Brown, Michael, Martin Carnoy, Elliott Currie, Troy Duster, David B. Oppenheimer, Marjorie Shultz, and David Wellman. *Whitewashing Race: The Myth of a Color-Blind Society.* Berkeley: University of California Press, 2003.

Browne, Irene, and Joya Misra. "The Intersection of Gender and Race in the Labor Market." *Annual Review of Sociology* 29 (2003): 487–513.

Bureau of Labor Statistics. "Household Data Annual Averages," 2006, table 10: Employed Persons by Occupation, Race, Hispanic, or Latino Ethnicity, and Sex. Available at ftp://ftp.bls.gov/pub/special.requests/lf/aa2006/aat10.txt.

Charles, Maria, and David B. Grusky. *Occupational Ghettos: The Worldwide Segregation of Women and Men.* Stanford, CA: Stanford University Press, 2004.

Chen, Anthony S. "Lives at the Center of the Periphery, Lives at the Periphery of the Center." *Gender and Society* 13, no. 5 (1999): 584–607.

Clear, Todd. *Imprisoning Communities: How Mass Incarceration Makes Disadvantaged Neighborhoods Worse.* New York: Oxford University Press, 2007.

Collins, Patricia Hill. *Black Feminist Thought: Knowledge, Consciousness, and the Politics of Empowerment.* New York: Routledge, 2000.

———. *Black Sexual Politics: African Americans, Gender, and the New Racism.* New York: Routledge, 2004.

Collins, Sharon M. *Black Corporate Executives: The Making and Breaking of a Black Middle Class.* Philadelphia: Temple University Press, 1997.

———. "The Marginalization of Black Executives." *Social Problems* 36, no. 4 (1989): 317–331.

Connell, Raewyn W. "Cool Guys, Swots, and Wimps: The Interplay of Masculinity and Education." *Oxford Review of Education* 15, no. 3 (1989): 291–303.

———. *Masculinities.* Berkeley: University of California Press, 1995.

Cose, Ellis. *The End of Anger.* New York: HarperCollins, 2011.

———. *The Rage of a Privileged Class.* New York: HarperCollins, 1993.

Davis, Angela Y. *Women, Race, and Class.* New York: Basic Books, 1981.

Dellinger, Kirsten. "Masculinities in Safe and Embattled Organizations: Accounting for Pornographic and Feminist Magazines." *Gender and Society* 18, no. 5 (2004): 545–566.

Durr, Marlese, and John R. Logan. "Racial Submarkets in Government Employment." *Sociological Forum* 12 (1997): 353–370.

Espiritu, Yen Le. *Asian American Women and Men: Labor, Laws, and Love.* Thousand Oaks, CA: Russell Sage, 1996.

Feagin, Joe R. *Racist America: Roots, Current Realities, and Future Reparations.* 2nd ed. New York: Routledge, 2010.

———. *Systemic Racism: A Theory of Oppression.* New York: Routledge, 2006.

Feagin, Joe R., and Melvin P. Sikes. *Living with Racism: The Black Middle-Class Experience.* Boston: Beacon Press, 1995.

Ferguson, Ann Arnett. *Bad Boys: Public Schools in the Making of Black Masculinity.* Ann Arbor: University of Michigan Press, 2001.

Floge, Lilian, and Deborah M. Merrill. "Tokenism Reconsidered: Male Nurses and Female Physicians in a Hospital Setting." *Social Forces* 64, no. 4 (1986): 925–947.

Frankenberg, Ruth. *White Women, Race Matters: The Social Construction of Whiteness.* Minneapolis: University of Minnesota Press, 1993.

Frazier, E. Franklin. *Black Bourgeoisie.* New York: Free Press, 1957.

Gilkes, Cheryl Townsend. "Building in Many Places: Multiple Commitments and Ideologies in Black Women's Community Work." In *Women and the Politics of Empowerment: Perspectives from Communities and Workplaces*, edited by Ann Bookman and Sandra Morgen, 53–76. Philadelphia: Temple University Press, 1988.

Goffman, Erving. *Stigma: Notes on the Management of Spoiled Identity*. New York: Simon and Schuster, 1963.

Harlow, Roxana. "'Race Doesn't Matter, But . . .': The Effect of Race on Professors' Experiences and Emotion Management in the Undergraduate College Classroom." *Social Psychology Quarterly* 66, no. 4 (2003): 348–363.

Harvey, William, and Eugene Anderson. *Minorities in Higher Education: 21st Annual Status Report*. Washington, DC: American Council of Education, 2005.

Hochschild, Arlie Russell. *The Managed Heart: Commercialization of Human Feeling*. Berkeley: University of California Press, 1983.

Hutchinson, Earl Ofari. *The Assassination of the Black Male Image*. New York: Simon and Schuster, 1997.

Jackson, Pamela B., Peggy A. Thoits, and Howard F. Taylor. "Composition of the Workplace and Psychological Well-Being: The Effects of Tokenism on America's Black Elite." *Social Forces* 74 (1995): 543–557.

Jones, Charisse, and Kumea Shorter-Gooden. *Shifting: The Double Lives of Black Women in America*. New York: HarperCollins, 2003.

Kang, Miliann. *The Managed Hand: Race, Gender, and the Body in Beauty Service Work*. Berkeley: University of California Press, 2010.

———. "The Managed Hand: The Commercialization of Bodies and Emotions in Korean Immigrant–Owned Nail Salons." *Gender and Society* 17 (2003): 820–839.

Kanter, Rosabeth Moss. *Men and Women of the Corporation*. New York: Basic Books, 1977.

Kaplan, Victoria. *Structural Inequality: Black Architects in the United States*. Lanham, MD: Rowman and Littlefield, 2006.

Kemp, Alice Abel. *Women's Work: Degraded and Devalued*. Englewood Cliffs, NJ: Prentice Hall, 1994.

Kimmel, Michael S. *Guyland: The Perilous World Where Boys Become Men*. New York: Harper, 2008.

———. *Manhood in America: A Cultural History*. New York: Oxford University Press, 2012.

———. "Masculinity as Homophobia: Fear, Shame, and Silence in the Construction of Gender Identity." In *Men and Masculinity: A Text Reader*, edited by Theodore F. Cohen, 29–41. Belmont, CA: Wadsworth Thomson Learning, 2001.

Kirschenman, Joleen, and Kathryn M. Neckerman. "'We'd Love to Hire Them, But . . .': The Meaning of Race for Employers." In *The Urban Underclass*, edited by Christopher Jencks and Paul E. Peterson, 203–232. Washington, DC: Brookings Institution, 1991.

Lacy, Karyn R. *Blue-Chip Black: Race, Class, and Status in the New Black Middle Class*. Berkeley: University of California Press, 2007.

Lamont, Michele. *The Dignity of Working Men: Morality and the Boundaries of Race, Class, and Immigration*. Cambridge, MA: Harvard University Press, 2000.

Leidner, Robin. *Fast Food, Fast Talk: Service Work and the Routinization of Everyday Life*. Berkeley: University of California Press, 1993.

Lerman, R., and E. Sorenson. "Father Involvement with Their Nonmarital Children: Patterns, Determinants, and Effects on Their Earnings." *Marriage and Family Review* 29 (2000): 137–158.

Lively, Kathryn. "Client Contact and Emotional Labor: Upsetting the Balance and Evening the Field." *Work and Occupations* 29, no. 2 (2002): 198–225.

Lopez, Steven H. "Emotional Labor and Organized Emotional Care: Conceptualizing Nursing Home Care Work." *Work and Occupations* 33, no. 2 (2006): 133–160.

Majors, Richard, and Janet M. Billson. *Cool Pose: The Dilemmas of Black Manhood in America*. New York: Lexington Books, 1992.

Martin, Susan E. "Police Force or Police Service? Gender and Emotional Labor." *Annals of the American Academy of Political and Social Science* 561, no. 1 (1999): 111–126.

McIntosh, Peggy. "White Privilege and Male Privilege: A Personal Account of Coming to See Correspondences through Work in Women's Studies." In *Race, Class, and Gender: An Anthology*, edited by Margaret L. Andersen and Patricia Hill Collins, 76–87. 2nd ed. Belmont, CA: Wadsworth, 1995.

Mirchandani, Kiran. "Challenging Racial Silences in Studies of Emotion Work: Contributions from Anti-racist Feminist Theory." *Organization Studies* 24, no. 5 (2003): 721–742.

Moore, Wendy Leo. *Reproducing Racism: White Space, Elite Law Schools, and Racial Inequality*. Lanham, MD: Rowman and Littlefield, 2008.

National Center for Health Statistics. *Health, United States, 2008*. Washington, DC: U.S. Government Printing Office, 2009. Available at http://www.cdc .gov/nchs/data/hus/hus08.pdf.

Nelson, Jennifer. *Women of Color and the Reproductive Rights Movement*. New York: New York University Press, 2003.

"Obama's Father's Day Speech," CNN, June 28, 2008. Available at http:// articles.cnn.com/2008-06-27/politics/obama.fathers.ay_1_foundation-black-children-rock?_s=PM:POLITICS.

Olsen, Lynne. *Freedom's Daughters: The Unsung Heroines of the Civil Rights Movement from 1830 to 1970*. New York: Scribner, 2001.

Paap, Kris. *Working Construction: Why White Working-Class Men Put Themselves and the Labor Movement in Harm's Way*. Ithaca, NY: Cornell University Press, 2006.

Pager, Devah. *Marked: Race, Crime, and Finding Work in an Era of Mass Incarceration*. Chicago: University of Chicago Press, 2007.

Pascoe, C. J. *Dude, You're a Fag! Masculinity and Sexuality in High School*. Berkeley: University of California Press, 2007.

Pierce, Jennifer L. *Gender Trials: Emotional Lives in Contemporary Law Firms*. Berkeley: University of California Press, 1995.

———. "Racing for Innocence: Whiteness, Corporate Culture, and the Backlash against Affirmative Action." In *White Out: The Continuing Significance of Racism*, edited by Ashley Doane and Eduardo Bonilla-Silva, 199–214. New York: Routledge, 2003.

Ridgeway, Cecilia. *Framed by Gender: How Gender Inequality Persists in the Modern World*. New York: Oxford University Press, 2011.

Roscigno, Vincent. *The Faces of Discrimination: How Race and Gender Impact Work and Home Lives*. Lanham, MD: Rowman and Littlefield, 2007.

Roth, Louise M. *Selling Women Short: Gender Inequality on Wall Street*. Princeton, NJ: Princeton University Press, 2006.

Royster, Deirdre A. *Race and the Invisible Hand: How White Networks Exclude Black Men from Blue-Collar Jobs*. Berkeley: University of California Press, 2003.

Shapiro, Thomas M. *The Hidden Costs of Being African American: How Wealth Perpetuates Inequality*. New York: Oxford University Press, 2004.

St. Jean, Yanick, and Joe Feagin. *Double Burden: Black Women and Everyday Racism*. Armonk, NY: M. E. Sharpe, 1998.

Susskind, Ron. *Confidence Men*. New York: HarperCollins, 2011.

Thierry, Mary Texiera. "'Who Protects and Serves Me?': A Case Study of Sexual Harassment of African American Women in One U.S. Law Enforcement Agency." *Gender and Society* 16, no. 4 (2002): 524–545.

Turco, Catherine J. "Cultural Foundations of Tokenism: Evidence from the Leveraged Buyout Industry." *American Sociological Review* 75, no. 6 (2010): 894–913.

U.S. Equal Employment Opportunity Commission. Executive Order 10925. March 6, 1961. Available at http://www.eeoc.gov/eeoc/history/35th/thelaw/eo-10925.html.

Weber, Lynne, and Elizabeth Higginbotham. "Black and White Professional-Managerial Women's Perceptions of Racism and Sexism in the Workplace." In *Women and Work: Exploring Race, Ethnicity, and Class*, edited by Elizabeth Higginbotham and Mary Romero, 153–175. Vol. 6. Thousand Oaks, CA: Russell Sage, 1997.

———. "Perceptions of Workplace Discrimination among Black and White Professional-Managerial Women." In *Latina and African American Women at Work*, edited by Irene Brown, 327–353. New York: Russell Sage, 1999.

Wharton, Amy. "The Psychosocial Consequences of Emotional Labor." *Annals of the American Academy of Political and Social Science* 561, no. 1 (1995): 158–176.

Williams, Christine L. "The Glass Escalator: Hidden Advantages for Men in the Female Professions." *Social Problems* 39, no. 3 (1992): 253–267.

———. *Still a Man's World: Men Who Do "Women's Work."* Berkeley: University of California Press, 1995.

Wilson, William Julius. *The Truly Disadvantaged: The Inner City, the Underclass, and Public Policy.* Chicago: University of Chicago Press, 1987.

Wingfield, Adia Harvey. "Are Some Emotions Marked 'Whites Only'? Racialized Feeling Rules in Professional Workplaces." *Social Problems* 57, no. 2 (2010): 251–268.

———. *Doing Business with Beauty: Black Women, Hair Salons, and the Racial Enclave Economy.* Lanham, MD: Rowman and Littlefield, 2008.

———. "Racializing the Glass Escalator: Reconsidering Men's Experiences with 'Women's Work.'" *Gender and Society* 23, no. 1 (2009): 5–26.

Wingfield, Adia Harvey, and Joe Feagin. *Yes We Can? White Racial Framing and the 2008 Presidential Campaign.* Lanham, MD: Rowman and Littlefield, 2009.

"The Wrong Man," *Washington Post*, June 25, 2006. Available at http://www .washingtonpost.com/wp-dyn/content/article/2006/06/24/AR200606240 1082.html.

Young, Alford. *The Minds of Marginalized Black Men.* Princeton, NJ: Princeton University Press, 2004.

Zinn, Maxine B., and Bonnie T. Dill. "Theorizing Differences from Multiracial Feminism." *Feminist Studies* 22, no. 2 (1996): 321–332.

Zweigenhaft, Richard L., and William G. Domhoff. *Blacks in the White Elite: Will the Progress Continue?* Lanham, MD: Rowman and Littlefield, 2003.

———. *Diversity in the Power Elite: How It Happened, Why It Matters.* Lanham, MD: Rowman and Littlefield, 2006.

Index

Adia Harvey Wingfield is Associate Professor of Sociology at Georgia State University. She is the author of *Changing Times for Black Professionals* and *Doing Business with Beauty: Black Women, Hair Salons, and the Racial Enclave Economy* and coauthor (with Joe Feagin) of *Yes We Can? White Racial Framing and the Obama Presidency.*